"Narda is doing a great service revealing her pa is not only fascinating and challenging, but als and solutions."

— **Charles Brandt**
Author of *The Irishman*

"Narda is a woman of passion, and her fire for life shines through on every page. Hard-won, this book is a must-read!"

— **Kathryn Kemp Guylay**
6 x bestselling author and founder of Make Everything Fun

"I read this straight through in one sitting–it's a wire-to-wire, page-to-page, non stop read. Put simply, this memoir is a spectacular piece of human experience, writing, and inspiration. Pitkethly fully engages her adventures and misadventures to lead us through the personal issues of our time. It reads like a bestseller for both women and men."

— **Carl Feldbaum**
Author of *Looking the Tiger in the Eye*

"Nardagani is a story of groping for meaning in mystery, and of turning toward life when faced with death and tragedy. Author Narda Pitkethly recalls her ever-changing childhood, her journey throughout the world in her young adult years, and her attempts at settling into conventional life in adulthood. At each phase, she faces challenges that twist her in unexpected ways, and cause her to dig deeply into herself to find a means to straighten her own path. Filled with equal measures of danger and redemption, this is a page-turner for anyone interested in persistence and resilience."

— **Helen Morgus**
Librarian at The Community Library, Ketchum, Idaho

"Insightful and inspirational. A beautifully written journey of self-discovery. Through despair to awakening with courage and a modicum of humor along the way."

— **Diana Anderson**
Author of *Migraine Protocol: Free Yourself From Headache Pain*

NARDAGANI

A MEMOIR

Finding Light in the Shadow
of a Brother's Disappearance

光

NARDA PITKETHLY

*May you always find
the light*

♡ Narda

Library of Congress Control Number: 2019917431
ISBN number 978-1-7342050-0-8 (paperback)
ISBN number 978-1-7342050-1-5 (E-book)

Edited by Carly Lunden, carly.a.lunden@gmail.com
Cover design by Zizi Iryaspraha, pagatana.com
Book interior and E-book design by Amit Dey, amitdey2528@gmail.com

Find Nardagani on Facebook-https://www.facebook.com/Nardagani/
Visit our website-https://www.nardagani.com/

This is a true story.

The people named have read and approved their inclusion in the book.

Some names have been changed to protect identities.

Sadieanne, Raleigh, Eric, and Jay—thank you for allowing me to delve so deeply into your characters. Your acceptance and understanding of my desire to tell my story was the support I needed to keep writing about the hardships and the triumphs.

I dedicate this book to you.

Table of Contents

Chapter 1

Lost

I will always remember the day I almost lost my mind.

I'm walking through frigid, thigh-deep water, one hundred yards into a dark mineshaft, completely alone. I'm searching the stagnant water with a stick, probing for a dead body, moving my stick methodically back and forth, from one rocky edge to the other. *When I find him, do I have the courage to reach out my hand and pull him to me?*

I feel certain he's here. I don't have the patience to wait for my friends to help. I'm alone. Alone with the cold, with the mud. And with the maddeningly slow pace of the search. I can't wait another moment to end this wretched misery. My foot feels an edge. Startled by knowing I've reached a drop-off, I stumble backwards, losing my balance. The stick disappears into the dark with a splash. Bursting into tears, my cries echo within the confines of the damp rock walls.

That was too close.

Pulling my legs through the deep water, I make my way back toward the entrance. Drained and weary, I come out of the mineshaft and into the light. My car is nearby, but with no towel or change of clothes. I pace and I sob. *What do I do now? With my wet clothes? With myself?*

Tomorrow, my friends will drain the mine with pumps to pull the water out. *Will I finally find Jay?* I weep, feeling as lost as my brother.

This living nightmare—the disappearance and search for my brother Jay—begins with a phone call. It's 3 p.m. on Monday, September 16th, 2001, and I'm home, working. I pick up on the first ring. It's Jenny, a dear friend of Jay's.

"Narda," she says. "Jay's gone!" Her voice is loud and full of panic.

"What are you talking about, Jenny? It's Monday. He's at work."

"No, he's not there," she says. "Cat called me 10 minutes ago and said Jay borrowed her Jeep to go to the store yesterday and never came back."

"What?" I ask, confused. "I'll call you back."

First I call Jay. No answer. I call again. Jay and I are close, so he always answers my call. I'm beginning to feel agitation, an edge of worry.

I call Jay's friend, Cat, next. She speaks quickly, with a slight tremble in her voice. "We partied pretty hard on Saturday night. Around five in the morning we got back to Jay's apartment. He'd locked himself out.

"Jay climbed onto the lower apartment's deck railing and tried to pull himself up onto his deck. He almost made it, but then he fell. His body hit the outdoor grill on the deck below and then his head hit the ground, hard. He was out for a long time. I knelt down and was shaking him, trying to get him to wake up, when the downstairs neighbor came out. He said he heard a loud noise, which must have been Jay hitting the grill. He had already run back into his house to call 911 when Jay came to. Jay insisted he was okay. He was adamant about not going to the emergency room. So we went to my place."

"You should have taken him to the hospital!" I say, too loudly. I knew Jay didn't have health insurance and that he refused to go to the doctor. My heart is beating like a hummingbird's.

Cat breathes deeply. "He wouldn't go, Narda. It rained all day, so we hung out on my couch, watching the news. Jay complained of a headache. I didn't know if it was from the partying or his fall, but it scared me.

"At 5 p.m. when the rain stopped, he borrowed my Jeep to go to the store."

Jay never returned. Someone had found Cat's Jeep Wrangler parked in front of a vacant home down the street from her place and called the police to report an unfamiliar vehicle.

I hang up the phone and immediately call the sheriff.

"Blaine County Sheriff's Department. Sergeant Taylor speaking. What's the nature of your call?"

I explain the story Cat has just told me. Sergeant Taylor tells me to bring an article of Jay's clothing and meet him at the house where the Jeep was abandoned.

Remembering that Jay left a jacket at my place a couple of nights before, I grab it off the hook on my way out the front door, jump in my car, and drive. I start calling Jay on his cell phone, over and over.

I realize Jay hasn't checked in with me for a couple of days. Usually we talk every day, if not twice or three times. He lives just down the street, so I'm used to seeing him nearly every day, too. He's my closest confidante. Last week, he was telling me about a woman he'd met and was thinking about asking out. I went over to his place to help him decide on what to wear for the occasion. After our years of ups and downs, these lighthearted moments are the times I cherish most.

Heading south from Ketchum on Highway 75, I drive about five miles, then turn quickly down a road that takes me into a subdivision called Gimlet. The homes here are large, each on a lot between one and five acres. The house I'm looking for is close to the Big Wood River.

I arrive before Sergeant Taylor and begin walking around, calling Jay's name. Wondering what state he might be in, I scour the river's edge in desperation.

When the sergeant arrives, he has a scent hound with him—a German shepherd. The dog eagerly smells Jay's jacket and begins sniffing everywhere. He can't seem to find a lead.

Sergeant Taylor is talking on his cell phone to Search and Rescue.

I can't believe this is happening.

In the hours that follow, everything barrels forward. News of Jay's disappearance spreads on the radio, by word of mouth, and through flyers with Jay's picture on them. Jay's closest friends have printed and plastered these all over town. A thorough manhunt is set to start the next morning.

At 8 a.m. on Tuesday, September 17, hundreds of people—locals, friends, neighbors—show up for a Search and Rescue operation. Almost all of them know Jay. The head of Search and Rescue assigns groups of 10 to search specific areas. I'm in the third group, in an open field. We walk, spread out in lines, fingertip to fingertip, hoping to find Jay lying in the grass or in the woods by the river.

I'm searching to a wild rhythm in my head, in my ears. It's the loud drumming of my heart. Thrum-pum, thrum-pum. Feeling that I will come upon his body any moment, grotesque images float on the edges of my consciousness. *Oh God, will I be the one to find him?*

I go from putting one foot in front of the other, to sobbing. My closest friends walk in my line on either side, bolstering me and chanting, "Here we are, Jay, come home. Here we are, Jay, come home."

Houses dot the borders of our corridor. When we come to a house in our path, our line separates, then we come back together, and the house falls behind us.

A small group has been instructed to knock on doors and ask people to check their homes and any outbuildings where Jay might have taken refuge.

With all the volunteers, we complete a search of Gimlet and the maximum perimeter—about six miles from north to south by about half a mile east to west—in just three days. We search the entire valley floor, and just a bit up onto the hillsides, which reach major elevations on either side of the valley.

Finally, on Thursday night, the search ends.

Exhausted, I go home and climb into bed. I toss and turn, overwrought. My mind won't let me go.

When I wake up, groggy, wondering about this strange nightmare, voicemails confirm it. My answering machine is filled with messages from friends and random people.

"Narda, we'll ride our horses out Eagle Creek this afternoon."

"Narda, I'll go out tomorrow on my ATV and search Indian Creek."

"Narda, my husband and I are hiking out Greenhorn Gulch with our dogs to look for Jay."

Starting to think strategically, I mark each of the areas on a master map and hang it on my living room wall. We continue to search every day. In the hills, out the canyons, and along the river that runs along the valley floor. Sometimes friends join me; other times I search alone.

Memories of growing up together and our tough-as-nails bond both sadden and distract me as I hike. Mental images threaten to overwhelm me. Jay had moved to Ketchum three years before so we could live in the same town. It was a blessing—the first time in our adult lives we'd had the opportunity to live so close, and we had been growing and deepening our relationship. I was 39 years old, Jay 42. We had discovered our shared love of being outside amidst the mountains and natural wonder of this place. We had spent much of our time together skiing, hiking, camping. We nurtured each other, buoying each other up. I can't seem to shake that gut-wrenching feeling that he's been taken from me. Or that I've been left behind.

A week after Jay's disappearance, the county sheriff, Walt Femling calls, asking me to come to the police station. "There's some evidence of foul play," he says. "Do you know a Kurt Brown?"

"Yes. He works at Chandler's Restaurant. He and Jay are friends."

"Kurt was at Cat's on Sunday, the day Jay disappeared," says Femling. "We questioned Kurt yesterday, but he says the same thing as Cat—that Jay borrowed the Jeep and left at 5 p.m. when the rain stopped. The thing is, though, we've had two people call in with odd stories from that day."

The sheriff had been contacted by a man who was the caretaker for a house on a large property in the Gimlet subdivision. It was raining hard on Sunday, so the man decided to check on the house's gutters to see if they were blocked with leaves.

As he drove up the hill to the house around three o'clock in the afternoon, he saw a peculiar sight. A man was driving down the private driveway in an open, white Jeep Wrangler. Rain was pouring down on the man's head. A bright yellow tarp hung out the back of the Jeep, flapping in the wind.

The driver fit Kurt's description.

Why was Kurt driving the Jeep in the rain? Could the tarp in the back have been covering Jay's body?

The sheriff then tells me about Dr. Fitsman, a local medic, whose home was near the house where the Jeep was discovered. Fitsman had called the station. He said he went outside when the rain stopped, and when he saw a man walking by, he waved. This was around 5 p.m. on Sunday. The doctor told police that the man tipped his head forward and away, picked up his pace, and moved quickly down the street. That man also fit Kurt's description.

"We're setting up a lie detector test for Kurt and Cat to take next week," Sheriff Femling tells me.

"And one more thing. When the Jeep was reported parked at the vacant house, we sent a patrolman out to check. The Jeep was soaked through and through. But, Kurt and Cat say that Jay left in the Jeep *after* the rain stopped."

That night, I dream that Jay is lost. He's in trouble with bad people and they've hidden him. He's been without food for days and experiencing tremendous physical pain. I'm searching everywhere. I beg them to tell me where he is. They laugh in my face.

I wake up, sweating.

The day of the lie detector test, I get a phone call that both Kurt and Cat have passed the test. One after the other, they stick to their story that Jay left in the Jeep at 5 p.m. *after* the rain had stopped. *What? How can this be?*

I can't rid myself of the image of Kurt driving Cat's Jeep with a yellow tarp hanging out the back and the rain pouring down on his head.

On Monday, October 1, a new panic sets in. Soon, it will snow. If we don't find Jay this month, we may never find him. I'm desperate.

I go to the bank and take all my money out of my savings account. I go to Cat's house and wave four thousand dollars in cash at her. I'm begging.

"Please, Cat. Take this money and tell me where Jay is. I won't tell anyone."

But it's no use. She just replies, flatly, "He left the house at 5 p.m. in my Jeep and never came back."

Our family comes together to create an advertisement. We run it in the local newspaper and make flyers. We post them all over town.

$25,000 REWARD
JAY PITKETHLY*

Oct 10, 2001

For information leading to Jay, or finding Jay

* Reward Expires Oct. 31, 2001

AGE: 42 HEIGHT: 5-11 WEIGHT: 190 HAIR/EYES: BROWN
CLOTHING: BLUE SHORTS, NAVY BLUE T-SHIRT, GRAY PARKA, BROWN SANDALS

Jay was last seen walking in the Gimlet area, south of Ketchum, Sept. 16 about 6 pm. He was on foot, without wallet or money. Earlier in the day he had a significant head injury and was knocked unconscious for several minutes. During the day he suffered headaches and mental confusion. Our sad conclusion is that Jay had bleeding in his brain from which he may have died.

ATTENTION: Hikers, Hunters, Bikers, Campers, Fisherman, Anybody Outdoors.

Please look carefully when you are outside. Check your property and your neighbors property. Check trails, river, creeks, and roadside areas. Please help us find Jay . . . before the snow falls!

The Pitkethly Family and Jenny Prentice

If you have information, contact:
Lieutenant Sage: 788-5555
Narda Pitkethly: 726-5160

> Narda has information on which areas have been searched.

If you are interested in becoming a volunteer for Blaine County Search and Rescue, please contact Lt. Greg Sage - the commander of Blaine County Search & Rescue at 788-5555.

Remember - Not all "mountain men" types are needed. People from all types of backgrounds are needed to run a crew of searches. Blaine County Search & Rescue is a non-profit organization run mostly by donations. Please send your tax-deductible donation to P.O. Box 98, Hailey, ID 83333.

Chapter 2

Supernatural

Mom and Jay were always close. They both had magnetic personalities, and people were easily drawn into their orbits. I'd be constantly amazed by the physical manifestation of this magnetism as people gathered around them at parties and social events. They even looked alike, with their wavy, dark brown hair, wide brown eyes and gentle smiles. It wasn't always like this, but as they grew older, each became compelling in a similar way.

After Jay's disappearance, my mother leaves no stone unturned. The pain of not knowing is relentless. In a flurry of research, she finds a psychic, a woman named Esmeralda.

Mom flies Esmeralda in from Phoenix, and I meet her at the airport, driving her directly to the Blaine County sheriff's office. I'm anxious, hoping that answers are forthcoming. We get out of my car and walk across the parking lot in silence. I open the door to the police station for her. She walks in, and I follow close behind. Immediately, Esmeralda looks at a female deputy and says, "There's a small boy standing next to you. He's saying he's okay."

Everyone is shocked. They know the deputy had a baby boy who died of SIDS two years earlier. *Could this psychic be for real?* I want to believe it.

After talking with the police, Esmeralda looks at a map of the area and points to the top of Trail Creek Summit. "Jay was taken here by some bad people who pushed him off the edge."

An officer escorts us into the back of a police car. He takes the wheel and Sergeant Taylor rides shotgun. We head out Trail Creek, which is a dirt road that drops off sharply on the valley side. There is no guardrail.

When we reach the summit, Esmeralda says, "We've gone too far."

We turn around and head back down.

Suddenly, Esmeralda shouts at the driver. "Stop! He's here!" We get out of the car and peer over the cliff edge. A few hardy trees have a secure foothold in jagged rock outcroppings. The valley floor is a thousand feet below. For two days, Search and Rescue does a perilous search with ropes, rappelling into the area. Jay is nowhere to be found.

Esmeralda returns to Phoenix.

A friend tells me she had a dream that Jay was on the hillside out Owl Creek. We take her dogs and search all day among the colorful aspens. The air is cold. I'm shaking; I can't get warm.

Please. We're running out of time. Where are you?

A local psychic named Gloria calls. "Jay died next to the river in Gimlet," she tells me. "His body is floating somewhere downstream." I go to Silver Creek Fishing Outfitters in Ketchum to rent waders. As I'm walking through the door, a man stops me. "You're the lady in the newspaper," he says.

With a sigh, I turn away and head to the back where they rent fishing gear.

Appearing in the newspaper is horrifying. *Where did they get that picture of me?*

I go home with the hip waders.

The next morning, I'm up at first light. I drive to Gimlet, park my car, and wade into the Big Wood River. It's late fall and the water is low.

The cottonwood trees rustle in the wind. I begin my journey, trudging along in search mode. The waders are heavy as I drag them through the water. But I am determined. *I will find him today.*

At about mile three, I realize I'm weak with hunger. I stop on a grassy bank to eat the apple and cheese in my backpack. It's a cool fall day, not a cloud in the sky. The sun kisses my face as I make a silent appeal to my brother. *Jay, this needs to end.* With my head in my hands, the tears flow easily.

I collect myself and call Gloria. "I'm about halfway to Hailey," I tell her.

She responds, "Be sure to check the channels flowing next to the river. I feel you are close to him now. Hang in there, he's there."

I need to rest before I continue my search. Pulling a jacket from my backpack, I lie back, tucking it behind my head.

In this quiet moment, stomach full and the crisp air warming, I allow myself a moment of peace. I allow thoughts and memories to float to the surface. *How did we get here? Where did this search really begin?*

Chapter 3

Growing Up

When we were kids, my older brother Jay was always getting into trouble. But no matter how deep the problem, he'd take on a mischievous look and say something irresistibly funny. Everyone would laugh. I learned at a very young age that I couldn't laugh and be mad at the same time. I also learned that my brother could find humor in any situation.

My earliest memories are of Jay and my other older brother, Dave, racing by me all day long, stopping to poke at me now and again. I thought Dave's name was "Boys," because whenever Mom yelled "Boys!" only Dave would come.

I was born in 1962, when Jay was three years old and Dave was five. Our family spent that summer in San Antonio, Texas, where our father was attending a camp for young Army doctors training to be soldiers. We rented a tiny one-room apartment in the back of a garage near the army base.

One afternoon, Jay went missing. There was a golf course across the street from where we lived, and the story goes that Dad went running around the fairways looking for him. Jay was nowhere to be found.

Finally, Dad got in the car and started driving around the neighborhood. He pulled up behind a parked police car and there was little Jay standing in the back seat. The shape of that three-year-old's head, his pointy ears and his buzz cut, were easily recognizable. Dad talked to the police officer, claimed his son, and headed home, this digression adding to the growing list of adventures in Jay's life.

When Jay was seven, it was 1966, and the country was in the thick of the Vietnam War. We were living in the barracks at Walter Reed National Military Medical Center, in Washington, D.C. Dad was in residency, training to be a neurosurgeon.

One day, President Johnson came to visit the wounded soldiers at the medical center. As he was leaving the hospital via a side entrance, Jay showed up at the doorway. My brother extended his right hand to the President, and the President shook it. The moment was caught on film by one of the cameramen for a local TV news station. That evening when we turned on the six o'clock news, there was Jay shaking hands with the President!

But when Jay was in third grade, something shifted.

I came home from school one day to find Mom yelling at him. "Ms. Tacter called today to say you're not doing your homework. Why not?"

Jay ran out of the house and didn't come home until very late that night.

A few days later, I was out on the playground and could see Jay over by the elementary school. He was surrounded by six traffic cones in a semicircle, and three boys were taunting him. My brother looked like a caged animal, scared and confused.

Jay began to hang out with the bad boys at school, and the fights at home worsened. Dad would insist that Jay sit on the couch to read with him. Jay would just stare at the book. As Dad pushed, things would escalate, often ending with Jay throwing the book across the room and running off.

Sometimes I would hear Jay crying in his room. I'd talk with him on the way to school in the morning. "What's up, Jay? You seem unhappy."

"I'm stupid," was his usual reply.

"No, you're not," I would argue.

"Yes, I am."

"No, you're not."

"Do *you* get pulled out of class every day to get *extra help*?" he would ask me. "*Why can't I read?*"

Chapter 4

Splinter Village

I'm five years old. I've been sitting on the porch all day, waiting for Mom. She's bringing a baby home from the hospital, her fourth. I've asked for a baby sister, because my two older brothers are mean. I'm wearing my favorite pink dress with a lacy collar and hem.

At Splinter Village, the nickname for the World War 1 army barracks where we live, the homes are all attached in a big U-shape, with a courtyard in the middle facing the street. In the distance, I can see Walter Reed Hospital where Dad works.

During breakfast, Dad had called from the hospital, "Your mom had the baby this morning while I was doing my rounds. She'll be home in a few hours. I've gotta run."

That afternoon, I recognize Mom in the distance as a speck leaving the hospital. Her black hair is piled high on her head and smoke is billowing up from her cigarette. A short, bright yellow dress shows her shapely legs. Only five feet tall, she always wears clogs for height. She turns onto the sidewalk. I see she's pushing a shopping cart. As she nears, I can see a blue blanket inside the steel basket. A *blue* blanket!

Mom comes through the open courtyard and up the path to our house. She looks tired.

"Hi, Narda. Meet your new baby brother, Tom."

Even though I'm disappointed, I take a peek under the blanket.

"He's so small," I say, touching his tiny fingers.

"Will you watch him? I need a drink." Mom walks past me and into the house.

Standing on the second step of the porch, I lean over and carefully take my new baby brother out of the shopping cart. I hold him in my arms. His tiny body is covered in a little yellow outfit. Only his hands and face are showing. He looks up at me with big blue eyes.

"I'll protect you," I whisper to him.

Watching where I'm walking, I carry him carefully to the far side of the porch, around the corner, and down five steps. There's a small opening in the wood siding. We go in. It's dark and damp. I set baby Tom down on the dirt. "Stay here, I'll be back."

Running into the house, I see Mom on the couch, drinking her cocktail.

"Where's the baby?" she asks, barely able to keep her eyes open.

"Oh, he's okay. I'm getting a candle to light up the fort I'm making under the porch. Can I take some of the towels out of the rag pile?"

"Fine. There's a bottle of milk in the fridge if he gets hungry."

Back at our fort, I make things cozy for the two of us. Some rocks on the ground hold our candle. Towels in a big square create a soft place to play. Holding Tom in my arms, I offer him the bottle. He drinks, never taking his eyes off me. Tom becomes my best friend. I love him with all my heart.

From then on, the only time Tom and I are apart is when I go to kindergarten for three hours every day.

Dave and Jay, my older brothers, are in charge of dropping me at my classroom in the morning on the way to theirs. Dad gives strict orders to cross the street only at the stoplight, two long blocks away. Jay and Dave argue.

"Nobody ever pays attention to the stoplight anyway, so why should we walk all the way up to the light when where we want to go is right across, over there?" Jay pleads, indicating the other side of the street.

"Because that's what Dad told us to do." Dave is a rule follower.

But Jay wins nearly every time. He doesn't want to walk to the stoplight. Standing on either side of me, my brothers grab my hands and we race across the six lanes on Georgia Avenue. Cars whiz by so close that I scream. Cars honk and I jump out of my skin.

If Mom or Dad knew what we were doing …

When school is over, I run the quarter mile to the stoplight, and then all the way home. Tom is usually in his crib. Mom is on the couch, either drinking her cocktail or sleeping.

When Tom is two weeks old, Mom seems to be better rested. Coming in the door after school, I find her back in the kitchen, working hard to make food for her four small children and a husband who is often exhausted after long hours at the hospital. She is also in the laundry room, folding mounds of laundry or unloading groceries or vacuuming. Then she's resting again.

Sometimes, though, Mom doesn't seem to have the energy to even notice me. It feels like she has more important things to do. She probably does.

Sometimes I follow her around, like a shadow, not wanting to bother her, just to be near her. When she puts on perfume, she smells like flowers, but usually she smells like cigarettes. When Mom isn't tired, she marches around purposefully from one activity to another. I never know which Mom I'll have—the Mom who's there or the Mom who isn't.

One day I ask her if she can teach me to ride a bike.

"I'm busy, maybe tomorrow," she says.

After several days of asking, I grow impatient. I prop baby Tom against a tree out back of Splinter Village. There's a wide concrete path with trees and bushes along the sides. The boys are still at school, so they won't know I borrowed one of their bikes. I sit on the seat, with one foot on the pedal and one foot on the ground, like they do.

"Okay Tom, here I go."

Pushing off, I immediately crash to the ground. My knee is scraped and bleeding. I back up the bike. "I'll do it this time."

I put my other foot on the pedal and push off, crashing again. Now both knees are scraped and bleeding. I line the bike up at the starting point again and say to Tom, "I've got it now."

Pushing off, I pedal once, twice, then veer off the concrete path into what we call the sticker bushes. Every part of my body hurts where thorns are poking me. Lying there, I'm stuck. Whenever I move just a little, the jabs get deeper.

I yell, "Help! Help me!"

I hear cars driving by on the courtyard side of the barracks. Gritting my teeth, I roll forward and out.

I keep trying to get the hang of the bike. I keep falling. Suddenly, the boys are there.

"Hey, get off my bike, you moron," Jay says, as he grabs it out of my hands and rides off.

Normally, we stay one year on each base, but here in D.C. we're going on two.

Huge cockroaches crawl over everything in Splinter Village. Mom is yelling on the phone. "Get rid of these cockroaches today! I can't take it anymore."

She bangs the phone down and mumbles, "Damn exterminators. Too big a problem? My goodness!"

Meanwhile, I'm upstairs with Tom. We've corralled three cockroaches in a little fort I've built. Looking across the hall, I see Dave playing with matches. He's burning the head off a toy man. He looks up, sees me watching, and throws the burning man under the bed. The torn underbelly of the bed immediately bursts into flames.

In a panic, I yell, "I'll get Mom!"

"No, don't tell!"

Dave lifts up the edge of the single bed and tries to put the flames out by beating them with a towel.

I think the flames are bigger now. "Dave, I'm scared. I'm getting Mom!"

"No, don't get Mom!"

The flames are definitely spreading.

"Go get Mom!"

Suddenly, the sprinkler in the ceiling is spraying water everywhere. Looking around, I see my room is getting wet and the hall is, too. I grab Tom and run downstairs. The sprinklers throughout the house are soaking everything. Mom screams from the kitchen, "Everyone get out of the house, NOW!"

Firemen come, but nobody can find a way to turn off the sprinkler system. We stand in the courtyard outside our house with a bunch of the neighbors, staring at the chaos. An hour later, they figure it out and the water stops. We go inside to see everything completely drenched. The ceiling sags. A fireman pokes a hole in the bulge overhead; a torrent of water gushes down.

Dad finally comes home and says, with resignation in his voice, "Well, there's nowhere else to go. We need to clean up this mess and tough it out."

Mom says, "Well, maybe all the cockroaches drowned." We all laugh. It's an odd sensation to laugh with the whole family. I feel surprisingly happy.

By the summer, Mom is pregnant again.

"Please Mom, I want a baby sister."

Nine months later, Richard is born.

Chapter 5

Mount Fuji

In the summer of 1970, I'm eight years old when transfer orders arrive for Dad. It's time to pack up again. We drive across the country in our brown station wagon and leave from the Port of Los Angeles for a two-week journey across the Pacific Ocean to Japan. Because Mom's afraid of flying, we travel by ship, compliments of the U.S. Army, aboard the SS President Cleveland. Everything goes on the ship, including our station wagon. Even our old dog Rosie.

As I stand on the railing high above the crowd on the dock, I watch confetti flying everywhere. *This is like a cruise ship.*

Exploring the huge ship is endless fun. It's six stories high. There are two tennis courts and two outdoor pools with people lounging in chairs, all holding cocktails with little umbrellas.

Every day before breakfast, Dad has us up and out on one of the many broad decks. It's sunny most mornings, but the air is cool enough for my ski hat. We walk three times around the ship, Dad carrying Richard in his arms. These mornings together make me feel like we are the loving family I have always wanted. Despite the massive ocean around me, I feel safe. Happy.

The days fly by. There's no shortage of activities with all the other families and kids on board. One afternoon there's a competition at the pool. The water sloshes back and forth with the motion of the ship. Dad, Dave, and Jay get in with the others. Everyone lines up on one side. When the cap gun goes off, they all swim underwater the length of the pool and back. The ones who come up for air are eliminated.

For the second round, eight men are still in the water. Everyone is crowding around the long, rectangular pool watching. When the cap gun fires, the men swim the length three times. Five of them surface and get out of the pool. Dad and two other men remain.

The controller shouts, "Gentlemen, five lengths of the pool!" Then he shoots the cap gun. Everyone is eager with anticipation as the three men dunk under the water and push off the side. One length, two, three… In the middle of the fourth lap, one of the men bursts up and then the other, gasping for air. Dad is now solo in the pool and continues swimming. Everyone's full attention is on him as we inhale when he touches the wall, turns and pushes off for another lap. We are riveted. *How long can he keep going?* At the end of the eighth lap, Dad touches the wall and surfaces to enormous cheers from the crowd.

Dad is tall and lean, with blond hair and blue eyes. He's soft spoken and has a gentle way about him—until it comes to competing in sports. He's most alive, most vibrant, when he's training and running races, which he often wins. At moments like these, and at the pool that day, I am so heart-burstingly proud of my dad.

Ten nights into this epic ocean experience, all the kids are told to go to a large room on the top deck. "Attention everyone! Find a beanbag or a seat and we will begin the movie. Tonight's feature film is *Willy Wonka & the Chocolate Factory*. There is a storm brewing, so please don't leave the room."

The movie is entertaining, until a boy gets sucked up from the chocolate pond into a clear tube. This frightens me. My tummy is upset from the rocking of the ship. I want my dad, and I head for the main door. When I open it, I'm immediately sucked out and across the ship's deck to the edge. As my small body nears the threshold, I grab for the railing. Somehow I'm able to maintain my position on the deck as the wind tries to sweep me overboard. Seeing the churning water below, I wonder how I'll ever get out of this.

I feel arms around my body and a voice shouting in the howling wind, "Let go. I've got you."

Slowly, fighting the storm, I'm pulled back across the deck and through a door, to the calm of the inside. I look up to see it's my brother, Dave. *Wow, my brother came out to save me.*

For three days the ship rocks and pounds its way through the squall. Everyone is throwing up. The smell of vomit makes it nearly impossible to sleep in our small cabin. When I do fall asleep, I have nightmares of Tom and Richard being blown over the edge of the ship and swallowed by the ocean. I'm not having fun anymore. *I can't wait to get off this boat.*

I still feel sick when we arrive in Japan. We load up the station wagon and drive away from the port. Thirty minutes later, Mom asks, "Where's Tom?"

There's an absolute panic as everyone realizes Tom isn't in the car. Dad takes the next exit and drives back to the port.

Three-year-old Tom is standing just inside the glass door at the port office. He's stoic as he sees us pull up. He pushes hard on the exit door, attempting to open it, but it's too heavy. No one inside helps. Dave jumps out of the car and runs to him. Tom gets in the car without a word or a tear, a look of acceptance on his face.

This is our crazy family.

We finally arrive at Camp Zama army base. Dave, Jay, and I hop out of the car. I get elbowed out of the way as Dave and Jay run ahead of me to a huge tree in the front yard. I follow along and clamber up the trunk.

Jay sees them first. His eyes dart to Dave, then to me. Gigantic colorful spiders are everywhere. They are *huge*. It's like a horror movie. We all scream and fall out of the tree onto one another and the pile of leaves below. We laugh loudly to dispel the fright.

Brushing the leaves off our clothes, we look up and are awestruck by a massive mountain covered in snow—it seems to be right in our backyard. The sides rise smoothly up to a flat top. We find out later that it's a volcano, Mount Fuji.

Mom yells from the house, "Hey kids, come help unpack!"

Japanese men bring in big moving boxes from our trailer. A man walks into my tiny room (typically a maid's quarters) with a box and says, "Hi."

I say "Hi" back.

He sets the box down. He comes into my room again and again. Every time he says "Hi," I respond "Hi." Not until later do I learn that the word "Hi" in Japanese means "yes," and also "yes?" as in "okay?"

The next day I go out into the yard to sit and gaze at Mount Fuji. It is truly stunning. The massive base stretches beyond view. I hold up my thumb and forefinger, framing this behemoth, trying to capture its grand size. It feels sacred, this place of pilgrimage. I feel like I'm on a pilgrimage, too.

There is a fence behind the house. Ever curious, I climb over it and carefully make my way down the steep hill to a village. I don't think twice about heading off on my own.

As people see me, their eyes grow wide, astonished to see a young blonde girl. They speak with excitement in a choppy, strange tongue. They bow to me rapidly. Shyly, I bow in return.

Two girls motion for me to follow them. The street is paved and very narrow. We three girls weave between the buildings. Some shops smell strongly of fish. Others sell vegetables and fruit. Restaurants have red and black Japanese lanterns lit up. As people enter, all the workers inside yell the same word in greeting, "I-da-shi-ma-se!"

We stop abruptly on the street in front of one particular door. The older girl turns the knob, and as the door opens, both girls yell, "Ta-dai-ma!" A lovely-looking young woman walks toward us, calling "Idashimase!"

She showers me with "ahhhs" and "ohhhs." Whatever she is saying becomes very high pitched when I follow the girls into the house. The girls stop me, giggle, and usher me back toward the door. They want me to take off my shoes. They motion me forward again, this time into their small and tidy home. The floors are covered with soft tatami bamboo mats, and the walls are white tissue paper. I follow them down a short hallway with small rooms on either side. There is very little furniture, mostly empty space.

Where are the beds?

The hallway opens up into a slightly larger room with a low table in the middle. The older girl slides open a door made of white tissue paper framed by two-by-two blonde-colored sticks. She pulls out some small pillows, places them on the floor around the table, and pats one for me. As we sit, another round of chuckles erupts. The younger girl points to her legs and then to mine. They are on their knees with their legs underneath them, whereas I'm sitting cross-legged. I learn later that Japanese women would never sit with their thighs open. I quickly change positions. It feels strange.

I look into the tiny kitchen. Only the mom fits into the small space. A little refrigerator sits on the counter, surrounded by shelves of dishes. A small porcelain sink is next to a two-burner cooktop. I don't see a dishwasher or a stove.

The mom brings over a tray with tea—it's warm and sweet. I point to myself and say, "Narda." The girls take turns saying "Naruda." They teach me that in Japanese almost every consonant is followed by a vowel, so my name must have a vowel following the "r." Their names are Himari and Akari.

A second tray is set on the table. Akari, the younger girl, places a steaming bowl in front of me; it has a fish head in it. Startled, I look into the other bowls, which have only pieces of fish. The girl points to the fish head in my bowl and says, "Hi?" raising her eyebrows. *Maybe they want me to eat this fish head.* I nod my head and dig in. They all bow and smile. I eat the fish soup—head, eyeballs, and all.

I sit up straighter, pleased that I managed to eat everything that was offered. The girls and I play for the rest of the day. They show me around their home and their village. Everyone we meet talks quickly with excitement, then they bow. I bow back. The girls delight in pointing to something and saying a word. As I repeat each word, Japanese begins to take on a rhythm in my mind.

When I return home, it's dark. Nobody notices me come in. Nobody noticed I was gone.

In the morning, I wake up early to make "hockey puck" candy for my new Japanese girlfriends, a favorite treat of my mom's design. First I heat the sugar and flavoring on the stove, then finish it off by baking it in a cupcake pan in our oven. It's not really hockey puck candy—it's just my favorite round hard candy in a cupcake tin, missing a few ingredients—but I call it that. I walk out to the yard and say good morning to Mount Fuji. Then, climbing over the fence, I scramble down the hill and find the park where I first met the girls. They're there, and happy to see me.

When I hand each of them a hockey puck, their eyes grow wide. They enjoy the candy with nods and "mms." I show them the other 10 in my bag. The girls lead me around the park. Each person we meet looks in the bag and says, "Hi." The girls look at me and say "Hi?" I answer "Hi." Before I know it, all the hockey pucks are replaced with yen, Japanese coins.

Because the typical Japanese family doesn't have an oven, my candy is unique. Every weekend I climb over the fence with a bag of pucks and meet my girlfriends at the park in the village. They accompany me around town as I trade candy for yen. When the candy is all sold, we play together until dark. I love playing with my Japanese girlfriends. I love my life in Japan and am tickled to have my first successful business at the age of eight.

Meanwhile, we hardly ever see Dad.

We're in Japan because of the Vietnam War, which is reaching a fever pitch. Dad explains over dinner, "Casualties are treated at a field hospital just behind the front lines (like the TV show *M*A*S*H*). Once patients are stabilized in Vietnam, they're flown to Japan, to the hospital down the road." Dad is the head neurosurgeon, and he has a partially trained neurosurgery resident from the Mayo Clinic handling a ward of a hundred beds, all filled with the wounded from Vietnam.

He looks tired all the time.

While Dad is overwhelmed by the war, Mom is flourishing. Japanese women teach classes on the army base, and sometimes I get to tag along with her. We learn to speak Japanese. We make sushi, fold origami and create beautiful Japanese flower arrangements called ikebana.

We've been in Japan about a month when one night, after dinner, it's obvious our dog Rosie is sick. She's an overweight black Lab. I don't remember how she came to be in our family. She has just become part of the chaos. Rather than spend the whole night worrying, Mom decides to take Rosie to the vet. She phones the main office on the base and they give her the name and phone number of a Japanese veterinarian. Mom calls, and with her broken Japanese she manages to get directions to his office. He'll wait for us to arrive.

We all pile into the station wagon: Mom, five children, and Rosie. Following the directions, we seem to be getting closer as we pass the described landmarks. But then, Mom is confused. It's getting dark. She says, "Oh well, if we get lost forever, at least we'll all be together."

We stop at a gas station for directions. Mom tries, in her best Japanese, to explain that our dog is sick. They can't understand. Besides, they're more interested in the American station wagon, the variety of children, and that we travel with our dog.

Mom mentions the veterinarian's name. Then they understand. Mom can say "How many street lights?" "Turn right." And "turn left." Remembering hand signals indicating numbers, we're on our way again.

At last we reach our goal, a little office with a small sign picturing a dog. It's in an alley with telephone poles on both sides. Mom stops our oversized station wagon in the middle of the road because there's not enough room for it in a parking space.

We all crowd into a tiny office that has an examination table in the middle. There are floor-to-ceiling shelves filled with cages of animals and large jars of unidentifiable things floating in liquid. The smell is part antiseptic, part fishy. The veterinarian looks at us and at the dog. I don't think he has ever seen such an entourage, certainly not in his office.

He looks around at the group of children aged one to fourteen, a mixture of blue eyes and brown eyes, blond hair and black hair, and asks, "Are these all your children?"

Mom nods.

"How did you get here?"

"I drove."

He shakes his head. Not many Japanese women drive.

He puts Rosie on the table to examine her, with all of us either helping or just getting in the way. He says he needs to give the dog a shot. I start to cry. Tom and Richard hide their faces. After the shot, the vet gives Mom some pills for the dog and says, "Next time, I'll come to you."

He asks brother Dave, "Did you bring this old dog all the way from the United States?"

We all nod.

Chapter 6

Pits Pita Pat Pitkethly

Staying in Japan would have been my choice. It was so different—a new discovery, day after day, that kept my mind and heart engaged. I felt unique there. Though the elementary school on the army base taught only basic Japanese, it was my girlfriends in the village who taught me how to have simple conversations in their language.

Japan had brought our family together for those couple of years. We were a team in a strange, new land. We needed to stick together. But in January 1972, we return to Fort Lewis, Washington, and Madigan Hospital, for Dad's last year in the Army. He resigns from active duty one year later.

I'm 10 years old. My older brothers, Jay and Dave, are always together, running around the woods, the neighborhood, and the town. My younger brothers, Tom and Richard, are also always together, usually in the yard or playing in the house. They're five and three. Tom wants to be with his little brother now that Richard is walking and talking.

So, what about me? Why am I always alone?

Looking in the mirror, I see a small, thin girl wearing glasses. Every few months, I get a new pair. Why? Because Jay breaks them, often when the glasses are still on my face.

The plain, shy girl in the mirror has scraggly blonde hair and green eyes. I have the same color hair as my dad's, but his eyes are blue. I don't feel special anymore. *If I were, I'd have friends,* I think to myself. But it's okay—I like playing by myself outside in the yard or in the nearby woods. I build homes for my little imaginary friends out of sticks and rocks. I take care of them. They like me.

Most non-humans like me: anything that crawls, walks, runs, slithers, swims, hops, creeps, flies or hides in a shell. I come home joyfully with strays off the streets, creatures from the ponds, fledglings that have dropped from their nests, and an assortment of wildlife I find under rocks, sliding down trees, and peeking out from under logs. And some creatures just join our household through the woodwork.

Jay torments me with his insatiable desire to kill everything I bring home.

Hands on my hips, staring directly into the eyes of my reflection, I say, "I want a real pet."

I still have money from selling my "hockey puck" candy in Japan. I hop on my bike and ride to the pet store. I emerge from the pet store with a small box, which holds a boy mouse, a girl mouse, and a play wheel. The container fits easily in the big basket on my handlebars. Riding home, I feel elated. My heart is bursting with love for these small creatures.

In a corner of our garage I find some cardboard boxes. With scissors and masking tape, I build my pets a home. I shred newspaper for their bedding. They like lettuce, carrots, and fresh water served in small Japanese bowls. I name the boy Nikki, because in Japanese Nikki means "baby boy." The girl is Ratto, because she acts like a big, strong rat.

I'm in fourth grade. At school, my teacher asks me to bring my pet mice in for everyone to see. The next morning, I walk to school with Nikki and Ratto in my pocket.

"May I hold Nikki?" asks a boy in my class.

"I want to hold Ratto!" says a tall girl. She giggles as Ratto scurries across her hands with her soft paws.

On the walk home from school, my face hurts from smiling so much. Suddenly, school feels more fun. People say hello and ask about Nikki and Ratto.

One day I tell the girl who sits next to me in class that Ratto is pregnant. The teacher asks if I'll bring the whole mouse family to school when the babies arrive.

Soon the pink babies are born. I carefully take the whole family to school in a cardboard box with lots of bedding. As I walk home after school, my face hurts from smiling, again. I like this feeling.

When the babies are 10 days old, they have soft white fur. My teacher and my classmates want me to bring them to school again. Skipping and twirling all the way home, I have never felt so happy.

Once home, I call out for Mom, excited to tell her about bringing the babies to school again. I automatically head to her room. She's in her bed, snoring. It smells like smoke and alcohol. *Sheesh, never mind.* I turn around and head towards my room.

From the bottom of the stairs, I can see my bedroom door is wide open. I always shut the door, so I know someone must have been inside. *Oh no.* My heart begins to pound. Reaching the mouse house I built, I see Nikki and Ratto are gone. Only the babies are there. Frantic, I head back up the stairs. Grabbing the handrail, I take two stairs at a time.

"Jay!"

He's in the kitchen, laughing so hard he can hardly talk. "In … the … woods," Jay says as he points out the window.

Jumping up and down, I shout, "I hate you! I hate you! I hate you!"

Desperate and furious, I bolt out the door. Across the street and 20 feet into the woods is a firepit where the boys often hang out. I go over there, suspecting the worst.

"Nikki!! Ratto!! Nikki … Ratto! Nikkkkiiiii, Ratttttoooo!"

I run around the area, stopping to look under bushes and inside logs. Nothing. I follow the path farther into the woods, searching.

Even at 10 years old, I'm remarkably organized. My whole body craves structure. Each item has a specific home, even my pets. Some items have a second home, like books in my bookbag. I know where each thing in my life is located. This gives me some peace in a family of chaos. Not knowing the exact whereabouts of Nikki and Ratto makes me despair. I feel like I've been kicked in the stomach, sucked into a downward spiral, like the Wicked Witch melting as she's doused with water.

After half an hour of hunting, I'm becoming undone. I head back to sit by the firepit and put my head in my hands, shaking with anger.

Then, I look up and my eye catches something far away—it's shiny. I run to it. Shocked, I stop in my tracks. There are two glass Coke bottles with the necks broken off. Nikki is in one bottle, Ratto is in the other. Both are floating in pee. They are dead.

I fall on the cold hard ground, crying and banging my fists into the dirt.

Oh no. What about the babies? Running away from the scene and back to the house, I stop in the kitchen for some milk and a tea towel. Sitting on my bedroom floor, dipping the corner of the rag into the milk, I hold it to each baby's mouth. *Come on you guys, drink!* By morning they are all dead. I'm consumed with sadness.

The cruelty of what Jay has done baffles me. I can't comprehend why he'd be so vicious to such sweet and innocent creatures. Not to mention doing something so hurtful to someone he's supposed to love. I feel a crack in my heart that leaves me reeling.

I stay locked in my room for three days. Each morning, Mom knocks on my door. "Narda, you'll be late for school."

"I don't feel well."

"Okay" is all she says.

Daytimes, I feel best reading books. The *Little House on the Prairie* series drops me into a family that loves and cares for one another. By evening, I'm starving. At night, when everyone is in bed, I go to the kitchen for crackers and apples. Back in bed, I have the same dream two nights in a row. I am running through the woods. Jay is chasing me with a huge knife. He's wearing a puffy red jacket. I run to our front yard and see Dave sitting in a chair, rocking back and forth with a look of shock on his face. Jay nearly catches up with me and I bolt into the garage.

Busting through the door, Jay grabs me and chops me into little pieces. Blood splatters everywhere.

I wake up, and then I remember Nikki and Ratto are gone.

Upon my return to school, the kids ask, "How are Nikki, Ratto, and the babies?"

"There was a fire and they all died." Numb, and feeling more awkward than ever, I fade into the woodwork.

By the next spring, we're in a new city and I'm at a new school. Dad has decided to retire from the military and open his own neurosurgery practice. We buy our very own home. I'm back in front of the mirror and thinking about pets again. *How about a dog? We had one before. Would Jay kill a dog?*

At dinner that night I announce, "I'm going to the animal shelter tomorrow after school, if anyone wants to join me. I'm getting a puppy!" Mom and Dad think this is a good idea—they rarely say no. Though, when I think about it, I realize they hardly ever say much of anything to me.

Taiho (pronounced Tie-ho) is the name of a famous Japanese Sumo wrestler. It's a tough name for a sweet puppy, but I want him to be strong, safe. Taiho is a beagle mix, with big floppy ears. All my brothers, including Jay, fall in love with him. We run around the yard playing and laughing together.

When Taiho is six months old, he sneaks out of the house and follows me to school. This becomes his habit. Some days, when I'm sitting in class, I look over to see Taiho, paws up on the sill, looking in the window. Everyone is thrilled when Taiho trots into the classroom with his head high and takes a seat at an empty desk in the front of the room. He even puts his paws across the top. The teacher has a camera and takes a picture. Taiho becomes our school mascot.

Then, one day, Taiho isn't at school.

When the last bell rings, I run all the way home. Pushing open the door, I call out: "Taiho!! Taihooo!!"

Dad is in the kitchen. *How odd—it's the middle of a school day.* My heart beats faster. He slowly turns his head toward me, and as our eyes meet, his face melts into guilt. I know something terrible has happened. He suddenly lunges for the phone. "Hello, this is Dr. Pitkethly. The dog I brought in this morning … I've changed my mind …"

There's a long pause. He hangs up the phone and puts his head in his hands.

I have that feeling of being kicked in the stomach again. Trembling with fear, I'm worried I may melt. There's panic in Dad's face and voice, the realization of a wrong, as if he's just now realized he's made an awful mistake. He did something to Taiho. *Where's Taiho?*

My parents had him put to sleep. Why? Because at the neighbors' fireworks display the night before, Taiho was scared and acting out. Dad had asked me to put him in the bedroom and to come back out to watch the fireworks show, so I did. Then, when the fireworks ended, I went to get him. He had knocked down some of Mom's and Dad's clothes. He had broken my parents' closet door and was in the corner of the closet, shaking and whimpering.

Mom came in and yelled at him, "Get out!!"

I don't know which of my parents made the decision, or whether my mom felt badly about it afterwards, or if they fully realized the damage done. But their brash reaction hardened something in me. It taught me a lesson. The people I love can hurt me. They're not to be trusted.

After losing Taiho, I stay locked in my bedroom for many days. The hopelessness and stomach ache hang on like a fever. All I want to do is sleep. Slowly, my sadness gives way to anger. I yell into my pillow, sobbing uncontrollably. I can't shake this terrible, crushing feeling of hate—toward my parents, my brothers, even little Tom.

Nobody comes around to check on me except Mom. Every morning she reminds me I am missing school. Nobody cares. I'm all alone at 10 years old. *Why would these people do these things to me?*

At school the next week, when my classmates ask about Taiho, I tell them he got hit by a car.

When I'm 11, we're firmly rooted in our own home that Mom and Dad have purchased in Kirkland, Washington. I'm once again yearning for friends, a companion—another creature that will love me as I love them. Ratto and Nikki didn't last. Neither did Taiho. *I gotta go bigger,* I think. *I'll get a horse!*

I ask my parents, and it's my good fortune that they consider the request. Maybe they sense that some permanent damage has been done, and they're eager to cover the wound. To my delight, they say they'll see about hiring someone to help us find a good horse. A month later, they speak the magic words. "We've found a horse for you, Narda. This weekend, we'll go see it." My heart expands.

The horse is *very* tall, 16.4 hands, and the color of honey. The woman who owns her is proud to recount the details of her physical beauty. "She's a dappled dun. See the dapples, the light checkered pattern on her belly? She is green broke, meaning new at knowing the rules. She's a smart horse. You'll be surprised at all she can do."

The horse's name is Pits Pita Pat. "Pits Pita Pat Pitkethly." *This is meant to be!*

We bring Pat home to live in the fenced pasture across the street, on our neighbor's property. She's the only horse in a 10-acre field with rolling hills and a small apple orchard on the far side. An old, dark barn sits near the neighbor's home.

Every day, when I get home from school, I call to her, "Pits Pita Pat Pitkethly!" and she comes running. Her eyes are so big and dreamy. Touching her huge soft neck with my small hand is the sweetest feeling in the world. I love to simply be with her, brushing her soft mane. Some days she walks behind me as I lead her to the barn for a bath with the hose. She stands patiently, enjoying the cool water and the massage I give her with my soapy hands.

"Here's a carrot for you. I have a story to read to you."

As I tap Pat between the ears, she lowers her head. I climb onto her neck. She lifts her head and I slide onto her back. I'm up high, bareback. She smells so good, full of nature. Holding onto her mane, I know she loves me, too.

I spend many hours with Pat, propping my book up on her large rump, reading to her, enjoying her whinnying, her walking around with me on top. We ride around the pasture, no bridle or saddle, just bareback and free. She goes the speed I want with my voice commands and the direction I desire through the pressure from my knees. When I ride Pat, nothing else in the world matters. Loneliness is replaced by freedom.

One day I stand up on Pat. She's bareback, I'm barefoot. I signal her to walk with a cluck of my tongue. This is easy.

Let's try trotting. I immediately fall off, landing on the ground with a thud. Pits Pita Pat nudges me with her nose and I climb back onto her neck. As she lifts her head, I rise up, then stand up again. She begins walking, then moves into a trot. With bent knees and purposeful breathing, I maintain my balance.

I make a sound like an extended kiss and Pat gallops. I fall. I climb back up on her neck and try again. And again, and again. This is a skill I master with many scrapes and bruises. Finally, I feel the joy of flying through the air on her back, like a girl at the circus.

Pat is my best friend for many years.

When it's nearly time for me to go off to college, I see the neighbor girl sitting on the fence watching me ride around the pasture.

"How does she know where to go without a bridle?" she hollers to me. Crista is 12 years old. She reminds me of myself at that age. I easily teach her to ride, and she falls in love with Pat. Who wouldn't? Crista's parents buy Pat from us.

I never see Pits Pita Pat again, but I trust she lived a long and happy life. When I think of her now, I feel a glow in my heart.

Chapter 7

High

It's Jay's 12th birthday and we live in Tacoma, Washington. I'm nine years old. There's a party at our home for Jay with some of his friends. When the party ends and everything's been cleaned, we all go to bed—except for Jay. He notices the liquor cabinet door ajar and an ornate bottle beckons him. He takes a sip. It tastes awful, but he notices the fabulous tingling in his body. He keeps drinking.

Overnight, Jay seems happier. He's talkative and laughs easily. He becomes the family jokester again, and everything seems lighter. He's not doing any better in school, but he laughs it off instead of shouting and running out of the house.

Jay frequently hits the liquor cabinet, and he has a way of draining the bottles methodically so Mom doesn't notice. She, too, frequents the liquor cabinet often.

By his 14th birthday, Jay has moved on to stronger things. Acid, and even heroin. One night, he's out on his bike. He's taken acid with his buddy and is too high to ride. Jay calls home from a downtown phone booth around midnight and twenty minutes later, Dad's there to pick him up. After loading Jay's bike into the back of the station wagon, he heads the vehicle toward home.

When they reach our neighborhood, Dad hits a cat that runs out in front of the car. He says to Jay, "Take a look, maybe we can save it."

Jay gets out and goes behind the car. Blood is spurting everywhere, and the cat's eyes are bulging. Jay jumps back in the car and barks, "Dad, it's dead. Let's go!"

Years later, when he describes the incident to me, he says it was scary but thrilling. It's a feeling Jay craves over and over again.

As time goes by, Jay becomes extremely moody. One day I come home from school and he's at the kitchen table. His eyes are red and he keeps smacking his lips awkwardly—his mouth is dry.

"Hi, how's it going?" I ask him.

"I'll show you how it's going," Jay says, and lunges at me. I jump back and run through the house, down the stairs and into my bedroom, slamming the door and quickly locking it. In a panic, I open the window and climb out. Just as my feet touch the ground, I see Jay. He's busted down the door. I'm faster than he is and bolt swiftly away.

I run like lightning out the side yard and down the street. When my feet slow to a stop, my whole body is shaking. Sobs escape uncontrollably from my mouth. I see a man go quickly from his porch into his house and shut the door. Shame heats my face.

Luckily, this time I got away.

That night, at dinner, the only comment from our parents is that it looks like we need a new door. How is it that I can feel embarrassed instead of standing up for myself?

The summer after Jay's sophomore year in high school, he ventures to Alaska to work on a fishing boat. It's a relief to have him gone for more than two months.

When he returns home, his arm muscles are huge. Jay takes one of Dad's beers out of the fridge and sits down for dinner.

"You're too young to drink," Dad declares.

"Oh yeah?" Jay roars, then suddenly grabs Dad and lifts him up nearly to the ceiling. Jay spins in a circle, with Dad horizontal in his hands.

I can't believe what I'm seeing.

Finally, Jay puts Dad down. Dad simply shakes his head and walks away.

The next morning, Jay is gone.

About a month later, Jay comes home. He's been at a drug-and-alcohol treatment center. He looks better. I'm surprised when he talks to me.

He says he's learned a lot about himself—"who I am and why I make the choices I do." He tells me he knows it's the 'cunning, baffling power' of alcohol over him. It's like a poison—but his body craves it. He can't allow himself even one sip; if he does, his craving will come back. He doesn't want his life to spin into chaos again. He knows he needs to make a major change. That his life depends on it.

Jay seems to be calm… so kind, as he shares his thoughts. This is a different Jay, a better Jay. I feel I can trust him, this new version of my brother. It's a good sensation. I want him to be this way, always.

At 17, Jay meets Victoria. She's smart. She adores being with Jay. She helps get him back on track, and he graduates with his class. The next year, the two of them go off to college at Central Washington University in Ellensburg. For the first time, I allow myself to believe that this new version of Jay might stick around.

For my brother, numbers have always been easier than letters, and he graduates with a degree in accounting. He even makes the Dean's List his last semester, to everyone's delight.

Jay and Victoria part ways when she moves to New York to find work in advertising and Jay goes to L.A. to make movies. It's not a bitter separation—they've both meant so much to each other. Now it's time to move on. Though he loves being on sets, he spends most of his time in an office doing accounting for the industry. We all breathe a sigh of relief. He's doing all right.

Chapter 8

My Dad

Like so many kids, when I was growing up I assumed that my parents—their identities, their motivations, their entire lives, even—were consumed entirely by me and my siblings. For many years, the idea of asking questions about their pasts didn't occur to me—and they didn't offer any hints.

In 1975, when I was in 8th grade, a school assignment to interview one of my parents opened the door to my dad's history. He kindly agreed to sit down with me.

My father, David Pitkethly, grew up in Roxbury, a small farming village in the Catskill Mountains of New York State. His father was a dedicated soldier and a WWII officer in Europe—an Army tank unit commander. My grandfather had spent his career in the military. The mold was Army, Army and more Army. Discipline, expectations and drive.

In 1952, Dad's sophomore year of high school, his parents decided to move to a warmer, larger city with more opportunities. His father, now a major, was assigned to Fort Sam Houston, in San Antonio, Texas. Dad met his future wife there, my mom, Susan Glass.

Mom and Dad were part of a group of kids on the post, all of whom went to Thomas Jefferson High School. Mom, one of the school's social leaders, decided that Dad would be her boyfriend, and so it was. Dad called himself "just a country bumpkin," but he and his younger brother had a car—a 1939 Plymouth, and later a 1934 Desoto Roadster with a rumble seat. They routinely drove as many friends to school as the car would hold.

Dad had never had a girlfriend, and when Mom showed interest, it felt good. Meanwhile, Mom's friend, Sandy, had her sights set on Dad's younger brother.

I ask Dad, "So you've dated Mom since the beginning of high school? You've never had another girlfriend and she's never had another boyfriend?"

"Yes, that's right."

I think wow, this is sad. They've only had this one relationship, and other than our time in Japan, they don't seem very happy together.

Mom's father, Colonel Albert Glass, was the chief of psychiatry at Brooke General Hospital, one of the U.S. Army's premier hospitals in Fort Sam Houston. Dad recalled him fondly. He loved and respected Albert Glass, he said. He told me he was the finest man he'd ever met. And because of him, he decided to go to medical school.

In 1954, after graduating from high school, Dad began his college years at Virginia Military Institute in Lexington, Virginia, his father's alma mater. Mom began college at Sweetbriar, only 20 miles from Lexington, so they were able to continue their courtship. Dad was a biology major and a runner on the cross-country and track teams. Always an athlete, he won many Southern Conference championships and qualified for the NCAA cross-country championship in 1956. Doing well in this race would make him an "All-American." He was keen to earn this stature. The event that year was held in East Lansing, Michigan, on the Michigan State University campus, the Monday after Thanksgiving.

He went off solo the morning before the race, driving from Lexington to Roanoke, Virginia, where he expected to catch a plane to Michigan. But the weather was bad; snow and wind kept the planes grounded. Dad boarded a train, hoping to get to East Lansing that night. When the train pulled into Cincinnati, Ohio, it was obvious he was not going to make it. He called a nearby airport and was told to take a taxi on over, a plane would be departing soon for Michigan.

When he arrived, he found no flights leaving for the rest of the night; they'd all been cancelled. He shared his sad tale with a ticket agent who took pity on him. Off duty at midnight, the agent drove Dad a hundred miles in a snowstorm, reaching the airport in Indianapolis in time for the 5:00 a.m. flight to Michigan.

Arriving 40 minutes before the race started, Dad quickly changed into his running gear in a Michigan State University dorm room. Sleep deprived, he ran the four-mile cross-country race and finished 15th, earning him the honor of NCAA "All-American" as a college junior.

As Dad tells me this story, tears well up in my eyes. I am so proud of my father. I think: He's not just competitive, he's *driven*. Even after all these years, the distinction remains one of the proudest moments of his life. I'm 12 years old, and I can't believe we haven't shared this memory until now. Is it just me, or do my brothers also not know this about our father?

Then there were his VMI years. "The first year they called us rats," he tells me. "'Hey rat, do this. Hey rat, do that.' We walked on the rat-line, a red stripe everywhere you went in the barracks. You had to walk stiffly at attention, chin in, chest out, shoulders back. Upper classmen would stop and harass you. They were ready to jump on any misstep with shouting and intimidation. Among many harassments were push-ups and holding a rifle straight out in front for as long as we could stand it.

"The VMI barracks had four floors with a courtyard in the middle. The rats—fourth classmen—lived on the top floor, third classmen on the third floor, and so on until the cadets in their last year had their rooms on the ground floor. All students were required to be in uniform at all times except when in their rooms. "We marched everywhere we went," he said. "To classes, meals, military drills, parades, and even to church on Sunday mornings."

Every Sunday there was a formal parade—dress uniform, dress shoes, brass and rifle, spit and polish. "We lined up outside the barracks in formation and marched to the parade field. The band played, orders were read. Then we marched back to the barracks. I didn't like it at all."

I'm curious about this Sunday ritual. "Did you go to church? I didn't know you were religious."

A laugh bursts out from Dad. "NO!" he practically shouts. "When you die, everything dies, your body, your brain—and there's nothing left."

"Oh, okay. Well, you just said you marched to church while at VMI."

"The way I solved the problem of not wanting to go to church was to join the last church, the one the farthest away. As cadets passed their church and peeled off, the group of cadets would get smaller. Eventually, there were so few that nobody seemed to notice where we went, so we just went to the local tavern instead of the church."

During Dad's junior year, Mom was beginning to express interest in a University of Virginia student. Dad was very upset. The Ring Finger Dance they'd agreed to attend together was rapidly approaching. It was a big deal, usually boasting famous bands and performers like Louis Armstrong.

"I went to the phone booth with my change, all set to call her and tell her our date was off. But I never made the call. She came to the dance and we went through the Ring Finger ceremony. It's like an engagement." It occurs to me how amazing it was that these seemingly small, micro-decisions could change the course of a life.

During Dad's third year at VMI, Mom got pregnant. With the reluctant approval of all four parents, they were married by a justice of the peace in Lexington. Mom wore a simple white dress, Dad his VMI uniform, and the witness was the wife of the justice of the peace. Marriage for a VMI cadet was grounds for dismissal, but luckily no one in authority ever found out. Another stroke of good fortune was that Dad had already applied and been accepted to medical school at Duke University.

"How was it telling your parents when Mom got pregnant?"

"Awkward. They were shocked and very disappointed, though your mom's mom, your Grandma Glass, was kind. Your mom's father, Albert, expected Susan would be a doctor, not a housewife." Only much later did I realize that this was to have implications stretching out for many years to come.

After Dad had completed three years at VMI and Mom a year-and-a-half at Sweetbriar, they moved into a small apartment in Durham, North Carolina. Dad started medical school on the 1st of October, 1957, and their first child, Dave, was born one week later. In Dad's words, "This was a very tough time for all three of us." They were totally unprepared for marriage and raising a child, especially on top of the rigors of medical school. Mom enrolled in the University of North Carolina part time, majoring in chemistry, and they did their best to raise Dave. "Your mom wanted to be a doctor. Both her younger brothers were becoming doctors. Susan always felt like she got a raw deal."

In August of 1959, their second child was born, Albert Jay Pitkethly, affectionately called "Jay." The family persevered and, in 1961, Dad received his medical degree and Mom received a B.A. in chemistry from the University of North Carolina.

"When Mom got her degree, did she feel good about herself?"

"Yes. But life at home with small children was busy. She knew this was the end of the line for her—that she'd never be a doctor."

They then moved to Denver, where Dad had an internship at Fitzsimons Army Hospital. I was born there on May 4th, 1962.

That summer we moved again—to San Antonio, Texas, for Dad's military training.

Listening to Dad, I begin to understand how challenging it must have been for my mom—for our whole family—with the chaos of move after move. He goes on, "Life for families in the Army is not easy. It was especially hard on your mom. She did all the packing, unpacking, then packing again. It seemed we would just get settled, and it was time to go to the next location. There was little time for her to relax and make friends."

There was little time for any of us to make friends.

He then tells me another story I've never heard before. Ever the problem solver, Dad tried to jury-rig my deep baby carriage into a place for me to sleep at night by getting a cardboard box to fill up the bottom and elevate me. One night I slid down between the box and the inside of the bassinet. Dad found me struggling to breathe and feared permanent damage. Ironic, since this happened just as he was applying for a neurosurgery residency at Walter Reed General Hospital. I'm taken aback by this confession—he had clearly held on to it for years, with no way to let it breathe. He seems almost relieved to share it with me.

There was only one opening per year at Walter Reed, and that year it was already filled. Committed soldier that he was, Dad took a place-holding job for one year as a volunteer for the 82nd Airborne Division at Fort Bragg, N.C. So, our growing family moved—yet again—to Fayetteville, N.C., and Dad became a member of the elite paratrooper unit. Then, in October 1962, Dad went to Fort Benning, Georgia, to begin four weeks of Jump School, the United States Army Airborne School.

As if October 1962 wasn't exciting enough, along came the Cuban Missile Crisis. And what first-line combat unit would be engaged to invade Cuba? Of course, the 82nd Airborne Division.

We continue the interview. "While I was at Jump School, I was in the best physical condition of my life. I could climb a 20-foot rope, hand over hand, do 20 pull-ups, do push-ups until told to stop, and carry heavy logs on my shoulders. It was pure torture! There's a short-cut to getting jump wings without going through four weeks of hell at Jump School, and that's to do a combat jump. My unit at Fort Bragg was in lockdown, confined to barracks and ready to jump into Cuba at a moment's notice. I contacted my battle group commander and asked him if I could rejoin our unit so that I could jump into Cuba. He assured me that the best place for me was at Fort Benning, so that is what I did until I had finished the four weeks of Jump School." But war with Cuba never came.

"How did you like jumping out of planes?" I ask him.

"I jumped out of planes, and helicopters, too! I loved watching the ground go by, then being the first one to jump. Falling through the air was about the only real quiet time I got," he said with a chuckle.

Dad spent one more year at Fort Bragg's Womack Army Hospital as a rotating surgical resident, then he was off to Walter Reed in Washington, D.C., for the remaining four years (1964-68) of his neurosurgery residency. In May of 1967, my brother, Tom, was born. It was a very busy time at Walter Reed, as large numbers of Vietnam War casualties began arriving.

In the summer of 1968, having completed his residency, Dad was assigned to Madigan Army Hospital in Fort Lewis, Washington. And so, we moved again, this time into a government house at Fort Lewis near the shores of American Lake. My fourth and youngest brother, Richard, was born at Madigan that November. It was our first taste of the Pacific Northwest, and we found it to be a wonderful place to live.

Our time in Fort Lewis was short-lived. Japan was the next big move, taking us to those two wonderful years in there. After our return, Dad finally retired from the Army and opened his neurosurgical practice near Seattle. That practice became Neurological Associates of Washington, which is still going strong today.

In 1997, Dad retired from his practice, and two years later he joined the faculty of the University of Washington Department of Neurological Surgery. Although he stopped seeing patients and performing surgeries in 2009, he continues to attend conferences and teach residents and medical students as a professor emeritus.

Because of this one chance assignment, a universe of stories was opened to me. I've developed a deep appreciation for my father and the choices he's made. He was simply doing what he thought best for himself and his family.

All those years, Mom raised us kids. I always felt her to be searching, what she wanted always just out of reach. Clearly, she wasn't content with her life as a housewife.

Her drinking got worse as the years went by. Dad tried to convince her to get counseling, but she refused. When things got really bad, like when Mom got into minor car accidents, she would go to an alcohol treatment center for a few weeks. She'd be gone, then suddenly she'd be home again, looking fresh. But this happy, well-rested Mom never lasted long.

Chapter 9

School

Thanks to Dad being in the Army, I change schools nearly every year. My grades are average—Cs, sometimes Bs. My mind drifts while the teacher drones. I think about being outside. At recess, I wander around the schoolyard perimeter. If there are woods anywhere near the schools, I find them. At lunch, I sit by myself and watch the others talking and laughing. Some kids get bullied, but nobody notices me. I don't really mind. Being shy, I like the solitude.

Once we are settled in Kirkland, Washington, I attend Juanita High School as a freshman. A boy approaches me one day in the lunch room. He has brown wavy hair and big brown eyes. "Hi," he says.

I look behind me, thinking he's talking to someone else. He smiles, then walks away.

A few days later, in the library, the same boy is suddenly in front of me.

"Hi," he says. "I'm Dan Strake. What's your name?"

"Narda Pitkethly," I say quietly.

"I've been watching you," he says with a bright smile. "Need any help with your studies? I'm pretty smart."

"No, thanks," I say shyly.

He backs up several steps, not taking his eyes off me. Then he turns and walks out the door.

Later that week, at the school assembly, I see the same boy. He's holding a microphone and standing in the middle of the gym. Bleachers rise up on both sides of the room and are filled with students. It turns out he's a senior and president of the student body. After opening the assembly, he hands the microphone to the principal, then walks toward the bleachers. He comes up the stairs and sits down next to me, smiling as he looks right into my eyes.

The next day in the lunchroom, there he is again. He sits down on my left, opens a brown paper bag and takes out a sandwich. "How are you today?" he asks me, taking a big bite.

"What's your name again?"

"Dan. You want to go to the football game on Saturday?"

"Maybe. Is it here at school?"

"Yeah, it's a home game."

We eat our lunch in silence for a while. Then he says, "I need to be early. I'm on the team. Come sit behind the players' bench. The game starts at 6:30."

More silence as we finish our lunch. When the bell rings, he turns to me. "I hope you can make it. See you then."

Nobody—and especially not a boy—has seemed to see me before. Something about Dan's persistence has my interest piqued.

On Saturday, I ride my bike to the football field behind the school. I choose a seat in the second row of the bleachers, behind the home team. Dan sees me; he waves and smiles. It turns out he's the quarterback. It's fun to watch him, although I'm not very familiar with the game. My brothers watch football at home on TV, but I don't hang around with them much.

Our team, the Juanita Rebels, wins 35 to 24.

From then on, Dan hangs out with me a lot. It's exciting and strange to have his attention. He asks a lot of questions and encourages me to talk.

"You need to talk if I'm going to get to know you. Think of intimacy as *in-to-me -see*."

Intimacy isn't something that comes to me naturally. It feels odd to open up. But I want to be close to Dan, so I talk.

Dan's father owns a car dealership, so he's always driving a new car. Before long, I'm going places with him. Never to my house—I'm afraid something embarrassing might happen with Mom's drinking or Jay's bullying, so we go to his. It's delightful to hang out at Dan's; his parents are kind to me. They live on Lake Washington. We swim, go waterskiing, share meals with his nice parents. It feels healthy and easy and sweet.

Dan's older brother, Ben, is the quarterback at his college in Southern California. Their team has made it to the Rose Bowl. Dan asks me to drive down to see the big game with him. "My dad says I can take one of the new Chevy vans off the lot for the trip."

I ask my parents. They say sure. Dave and Jay ask if they can come, too. Suddenly, my older brothers are really nice to me. Dan invites them along for the ride.

It's a wonderful trip. We spend three days in sunny Southern California and all four of us click. The football game is fun, even though Ben's team is not victorious.

Around this time, my relationship with Jay begins to shift. He goes from being a terror to being my protector. I feel more his equal, whereas before I was inferior in his eyes. Maybe it's that he sees me differently. Or maybe I've relaxed, become easier to get close to. Either way, I'm thrilled with this tentative new bond.

One evening on the drive home, Dave and Jay decide to stay in a motel. Dan and I stay in the van in the parking lot. That night, awkwardly but happily, I become a woman.

Dan and I are together the rest of the school year. Summer comes, and though he questions my motives, I continue to keep him away from my dysfunctional family. I want to protect this precious balance we've created, wrapped in our own cocoon, away from the shame I feel about my family.

In the fall, Dan goes off to Georgetown University, which feels about a million miles away. Our separation is painful, but inevitable.

I've had the best year of my life, and for that I'll always be grateful. We say goodbye. "See you later, alligator."

Starting my sophomore year, I feel changed. Because of the time with Dan, I experienced love. Feeling safe with another human being was new to me, as was someone's genuine interest in me. Dan changed how I thought about myself, and in one year I went from being shy and withdrawn to confident and lovable, even interesting.

Now, at age fifteen, the feeling of love in me is a deep kind of knowing, something to lean on. This is the beginning of spirituality and a trust that there is a way for deeper connection.

Chapter 10

Glassblowing

It's 1979 and I'm a senior in high school. Grades have improved somewhat since being with Dan—Bs and sometimes As. Math, science and social studies are coming more easily, but my favorite classes are art and shop. I feel challenged, but not in ways that feel overwhelming. Working with wood is a stimulating skill to learn. I like using my hands, I like creating things.

Jay's friends have begun to take notice of his younger sister, me. I realize I'm no longer the odd, lonely girl looking in the mirror. I'm a young woman with blonde hair that falls to my shoulders, a slender figure, and an engaging smile, similar to Jay's.

It's a delightful surprise when suddenly Jay is asking if I'd like to join them at parties in town. He's charming and attracts the attention of girls easily. He's also drinking again, but nothing terrible is happening because of it. Things seem fairly under control.

Dad says I can go anywhere I like for college. But my family isn't any help figuring out where I want to go. They're all too busy.

I have no idea where to apply. But somehow, I stumble upon some information about Smith College, a small liberal arts women's college in western Massachusetts. A school far from my family sounds intriguing, but my grades aren't good enough. Fortunately, they have an intake program. If I'm doing well after one year at the nearby University of Massachusetts, I can enroll in classes at Smith.

The day I leave home for college is the best day of my life. Getting on the plane, literally flying solo, gives me a true sense of freedom. This can be a new beginning, I tell myself. A chance for reinvention.

I arrive at UMass in the fall of 1980. My plan is to complete a year at the university, then move on to the much-smaller Smith College.

The UMass campus is huge. Finding my dorm is an adventure in itself. As I walk along the smooth cement pathways from one brick building to the next, I'm in awe of my surroundings: new sights, new faces and gorgeous fall colors in the trees that grace the walkways.

My dorm room is on the 13th floor of a 22-story building called Washington Tower. This is my first disappointment. Anxiety creeps in; I don't want to live 13 stories up. If anything goes wrong, I'm too far off the ground to manage. Like always, I prefer to be closer to the earth. Entering the elevator, I begin to feel trapped. I'm suffocating inside—a feeling that grows stronger with each rising level. Room 1333 is a long walk down a narrow cinderblock hallway.

I knock lightly on the door, then open it. It smells of stinky socks. The room is cold and cramped, with four concrete walls.

My roommate is lying on her bed. She has long, straight black hair.

"Hi, I'm Narda. Nice to meet you."

"I've taken the lower bunk" is all she says. She doesn't make eye contact.

As I walk over to the far empty closet, I hear her leave the room behind me. She doesn't return until late that night.

Classes start the next morning. They're held in huge auditoriums. Teachers wear microphones so the 300-plus students can hear them. Walking from class to class, I'm a little fish in a sea of 30,000 students. Surrounded by so many people, I'm still alone. It's good I enjoy my own company.

My first Saturday on campus, I'm startled awake in the middle of the night by a piercing sound. It's a fire alarm. Trying to protect my ears, I dress quickly. Someone bangs on the door.

"Get out of the building, now!"

Things have really gone wrong!

I grab my coat and race down the hall. The elevator is not an option. Throngs of students rush down the many stairs to the ground floor and out into the cold, dark night. A large crowd mills around outside the building. Finally, the loud alarm stops. My ears hurt, my head hurts and I need to lie down. The "all clear" sounds, and everyone goes back into the building. There's a long line at the elevator. I climb the 13 floors up to my room.

The following Saturday, the fire alarm blares again. I'm startled awake, get dressed and hustle down the stairwell, the shrill noise unnerves me. This happens every Saturday night for the entire semester. It seems they can't catch the person pulling the alarm. *What am I doing here?* The classes feel impersonal. And although I've met a few nice people on the 13th floor, it just doesn't feel good.

When the leaves fall at the end of the first semester, I go home to Seattle, knowing I won't be back. I decide to enroll at the University of Washington, and my plans of attending Smith College disappear. I feel devastated, but I'm also somehow relieved. I chose a school as far away from home as possible, but distance failed to spark the reinvention I'd been looking for.

In the end, it's good to be back in the Northwest and close to my family as we go through a tremendous shift. My parents have decided to get a divorce, which I already felt was a long time coming. They say they stayed together for the kids. *You didn't do me any favors.*

Dad moves into a condo. Mom stays in the family home and seems to be pulling herself together. She's gone back to her maiden name, Glass, and she stops drinking. This is the first time I've ever seen her really take control of her life. She's not happy, but she's making good decisions. I feel hopeful.

During the holidays, I search the newspaper in the hopes of finding a room to rent before classes begin in January. On New Year's Day, I knock on the front door of a three-story Victorian home just off the UW campus. There's no response, so I open it, calling out, "Hello, anybody here?"

A short, red-haired man walks toward me. He sweetly says, "Hi, I'm Ned. You must be Narda. Cindy said you'd be stopping by to see our place. The open room is upstairs. Follow me." The room is fresh, clean, and has a window looking out onto the quiet neighborhood.

What a relief. "I'll take it."

There are six of us living in this house. Everyone is kind and respectful. I become fast friends with Ned and his girlfriend, Nancy. They introduce me to yoga, and we drink smoothies with fresh greens.

The winter in Seattle is cold and gray. I spend much of my time in the art department on the south edge of the campus. To find creativity in the world of art, I must slow down, breathe, and connect with my inner self. I enjoy making paper, creating decorative books with blank pages inside, and doing batik the most.

As my junior year comes to a close, it's clear I've exhausted most of the classes that interest me. But, my advisor has a solution. He suggests I take a glassblowing class, off-campus at Pratt Fine Arts Center, close to downtown. "I'll review your work every month and you will earn credits toward graduation next year," he says.

When I call Pratt Fine Arts Center, they say I need a partner. All my artist friends are busy. Plus, it's an expensive class.

One afternoon, I'm on the phone with Mom.

"I'm not sure what to do. Nobody will sign up to take the beginner glassblowing class with me."

"I'll do it with you, if you really need a partner," Mom suggests.

"You'd do it?" I say, surprised.

"Sure, I have a lot of time on my hands right now."

"Okay, great. I'll sign us up. Thanks, Mom."

Mom picks me up and we drive to Seattle's Central District. Neither of us has ever been to this part of town before. Pratt is located high up on a hill overlooking the Seattle Kingdome Sports Center. I can see Puget Sound in the distance. Mom parks the car in the lot behind a low brick building. I open the car door and air rushes in with a delicious aroma of something thick and sweet. On the next block, a sign looms high for the Wonder Bread factory.

Our glass instructor is Steve Harman. He looks 40-something, with sandy blond hair and kind eyes that shine from behind his round-rimmed glasses. There are six of us students. We're assigned in pairs to an odd-looking bench with an assortment of metal and wooden tools hanging down the front side.

Steve explains a bit about the tools and says, "Put on your sunglasses and gather around." He opens the furnace, hot with molten glass. The heat is intense. At 2,200 degrees Fahrenheit, the blast of air from the furnace takes my breath away.

"This is where you'll gather glass onto your blowpipe. Your assistant will open the door and shield your hands from the heat as best he can with these two wooden paddles."

He opens the door again to demonstrate. This time he sets the blowpipe inside the ledge of the furnace. Dipping the end of the steel pipe into the thick liquid, he rotates one full turn, then two. Quickly and carefully, so as not to drip glass on the edge of the furnace, he lifts the fiery ball out, continuously rotating the pipe.

Holding the blowpipe toward us, he says, "See how fluid it is? You need to keep the pipe turning. Point it toward the ceiling and the glass will flow toward you. Point it toward the floor and the glass will get longer, easily out of control. Keep the pipe horizontal and bring your piece to the bench, like this."

Steve sits and carefully sets the pipe on the metal arms of a workbench, always rotating. Then he pulls a wooden-handled tool out from a bucket of water. It's a blackened wooden block, rounded-out from shaping hot forms again and again. As he rolls the ball of glass into the block, water sizzles and pops.

"Is that piece of newspaper a tool?" I ask with a laugh, gesturing toward the wet square under his arm.

"Yes—my favorite. I'll show you how to make one. You have to fold newspaper, tuck in the edge and puncture it with holes. Then soak it overnight, holding it down with a wooden block at the bottom of a bucket filled with water." He takes the square of paper in his hand and shapes the fluid blob.

"I can feel and shape my piece," he says as smoke billows up.

"It's so hot, "Mom says. "Can I wear gloves to protect my hands?"

"No, you'd be burned before you could get the glove off. The sweat on your hand will turn to steam very quickly if you accidently touch something that's a thousand degrees."

Taking turns, we experiment working with the glass while our assistant does his best to shield us from the heat with the paddles.

At the end of class, Mom says, "I'm sorry, Narda. It's just too hot for me."

"Oh Mom, hang in there for one more class. I need you. Please?"

She does.

In the second class, we learn to use a tool called "Jacks." We make the neck of our glass piece with the pointy end of the Jacks. While using the opposite end to flatten the molten glass, I accidentally touch the hot tip to my bare arm. "Ouch!" I yelp.

Steve rushes over with a soothing ointment from the refrigerator. "This aloe works pretty well for burns. It's going to smart for a while. You won't die from glassblowing, but you'll certainly get burned from time to time."

At the end of the second session, I say to Mom, "You're right, this is too hot. We don't have to do the third class."

"Actually, it didn't seem so bad this time. Let's stick with it," she says with a twinkle in her eye.

In the third class, we learn how to use color. Mom and I are exhilarated. When Steve invites us to the next-level course, we say simultaneously, "Sounds great!"

We become known as the mother-daughter team. Forming this team seems to spark something for us, a tightly-knit relationship that we've never had before. Our common passion binds us as we share this time together, talking about everything. It's as if a dam has broken—we're making up for lost time.

Paperweights are our first creations. Then we progress to cups, bowls and vases. I love making functional art. I start reading up on glass experts.

Summer comes, and Mom and I sign up for a three-week intensive course at a school north of Seattle called Pilchuck Glass School, in the North Cascade Mountains. The two-hour drive is beautiful. As we approach the school, the road becomes dirt. In the middle of a pond, there's a large glass sculpture. Cabins dot the hillside. We park the car in a gravel lot and head toward a small square building; wooden shingles adorn the entire structure. A friendly young woman greets us. The place looks promising, inviting.

"Welcome to Pilchuck. You'll be in cabin number four." She gives us a meal schedule and says there'll be an orientation at dinner in the lodge, down the path to the left. She points out the hot shop in the field behind us and hands us a schedule of the classes. "We blow around the clock in four-hour increments, and everyone has an opportunity to work in the hot shop each day. During the first week, your blow time is 2 a.m. to 6 a.m."

What? In the middle of the night?

Searching for cabin number four, we pass unique sculptures placed on lawns and at the edge of the forest. As people stroll by, they stop and introduce themselves. The energy is high and the sky is blue. There's a gentle breeze with a scent of wildflowers.

That night, after dinner, everyone heads to the hot shop. It's a large, open, wooden structure with an octagonal roof. Four glassblowing benches face outward, framing the interior space.

I'm amazed when Dale Chihuly steps into the center of the room. I never dreamed he'd actually be here—he's the most famous glass artist in America. We learn that Dale built this school just nine years before our arrival. His magnificent glasswork and keen marketing sense have fueled his popularity, and he's well on his way to becoming the most famous glass artist in the entire world.

Dale immediately gets everyone's attention. "Thank you for coming to Pilchuck. We have two glass artists who will perform demos tonight. They need no introduction."

William Morris and Rich Royal, also famous in the glass world, walk to the center of the shop. My jaw drops—I'm thrilled to be in the presence of such greatness, such talent. I learned about these famous glassblowers soon after Mom and I began blowing glass at Pratt.

They work for several hours, forming molten glass into spectacular art. I'm completely captivated, then surprised to discover it's already midnight.

Mom and I go back to our cabin to rest. But I'm too full of energy, and decide to take a walk. The moon shines just enough to light my way as I follow the paths around Pilchuck. *Wow, how did I get so lucky?*

At 2 a.m., we enter the shop and begin blowing. Three pairs occupy the other benches. The excitement is palpable as we work, immersed in the dead of night. It's an eerie sensation to be creating art with molten glass while everyone else sleeps. By 6 a.m., I'm exhausted. I sleep soundly until breakfast, two hours later.

The first week goes by in a dream-like continuum. Mom goes to bed right after dinner to rest before our 2 a.m. blow time. I stay up, chatting with the other artists, and sleep only from 6 a.m. to 8 a.m. I'm on a glass-blowing high.

The second week we get a daytime shift, but I stay on my two-hour sleep schedule. There are people up all night, everywhere. They blow glass or talk about art on the grass outside the hot shop. I don't want to miss a thing. I recall a story about gurus in India who sleep only a couple of hours each night. I, too, can do it now!

This surreal experience continues into a third week, and Mom and I are forming a deeper bond every day. It feels like I've found a long-lost friend. We've known each other my whole life, yet we've never experienced intimacy. She often apologizes, saying she wishes she could go back and be a better mother. I wish that too. How different would I be? Would I love myself, because I felt loved? Mom was lost, searching for her own contentment, and with my help she has finally found it—the world of glassblowing.

This ease and comfort inspires me to break out of my usual functional art. Instead, I make sculptural pieces—tall, reedy shapes and spheres—for my garden at the house I share with my college room-mates. When the time comes to return home, I'm sad to leave this magical place and the wonderful people we've met. Many of us vow to return next year.

Mom and I drive through the woods onto the highway. A couple of chatty hours later, we arrive at her home in Kirkland. My youngest brother, Richard, greets us as we pull in the driveway. We tell him excitedly about our amazing three weeks.

"Hey," he says, caught up in our enthusiasm, "I want to be a glassblower!"

"You'd love it," says Mom. "Narda has to focus on school so I need a partner."

I love to blow glass, but a break sounds good. The mother-son team is born!

While Mom continues to hone her glassblowing skills at Pratt Fine Arts, she sends Richard off to various glassblowing schools: Pratt, Pilchuck and Appalachian Center for Craft at Tennessee Tech.

In time, though, Mom begins to feel hassled by the frequent drives into Seattle. She partners with a fellow glassblower and friend who lives a mile up the road in Kirkland. Together they build a glassblowing studio in her second garage bay.

When Richard returns to Kirkland from learning how to blow glass, he and Mom start working together. Mom decides to start a company, which she names The Glass Kingdom. The name reflects her destiny, being born Susan Glass, and this new identity. It also reveals that she is building a kingdom, a passion shared with two of her children. Mom is crafting the world she wants to live in, at last.

Chapter 11

Turning Japanese

In 1984, I earn my B.A. in art from the University of Washington. For graduation, Mom and Dad give me a precious gift—an open-ended, round-trip ticket to London and $2,000 spending money. I'm buzzing with excitement. The first thing I buy is a Eurail train pass, good for two months. With everything I need in a backpack, I fly from Seattle to Heathrow, England.

That familiar feeling of freedom that comes with being solo settles back in, just when I first headed off to college. Now I'm on a plane to a place I've never been with no agenda. I love it. I wonder how long I can last with the money I have in traveler's checks.

I travel through Europe, staying in youth hostels and meeting dynamic people who intrigue me. After two months, my Eurail pass has expired. I'm in Italy. My funds are getting low. I decide to check out Greece.

I hop from island to island by boat. The islands are magnificent, but the boat rides make me seasick. Back in Athens, I walk into a student travel office. "I need to get back to London, but I want to see more along the way. I don't want to ride on a boat and I don't have a lot of money. What do you suggest?"

"The cheapest flight is to Istanbul."

"That'll work."

Istanbul is the most unusual place in all my travels, with more than 14 million people and a deep and colorful culture. I'm fascinated by it. Majestic, sparkling mosques dot the city. I'm moved by the "Bong!" calling worshippers to prayer five times each day. After two weeks, I board a bus to Salzburg, Austria. It's a lively, 44-hour ride with mostly Turkish people. We dance in the aisle to Turkish music, share food, and I learn to play backgammon.

I spend many hours on this journey sitting and staring out the window. I'm 22 and having the adventure of a lifetime.

Once in Salzburg, I'm out of money, with 800 miles between me and the London airport. Realizing my options are limited, I stick out my thumb and hitchhike across Austria, Switzerland and France. Just north of Paris, I hitch a ride with a trucker. He hides me in his back seat for the boat ride over the English Channel, so I ride for free; then he tells me how to sneak onto a train to get to Heathrow airport. Finally, on the plane, I eat every morsel of food offered, then ask for more.

The day after my return from Europe, I run into Ned, my college friend, in a coffee shop in downtown Seattle. I haven't seen him since we lived in the three-story Victorian home just off the UW campus.

Surprised and happy to see each other, we sit down to catch up. He tells me all about Japan, where he's been living since graduation. I return the favor with tales from Europe.

"Are you happy to be home?" he asks.

"No, not actually," I tell him. "All I want to do is keep traveling."

"Why don't you join me in Japan?" he suggests. "You can stay with me until you find a place. Get yourself a motorcycle license and a one-way plane ticket."

The two years my family spent in Japan, living at Camp Zama army base, are some of my fondest memories, so going back with Ned sounds appealing. I borrow money from Dad for the ticket, promising to pay him back. The motorcycle license is easy to get—just a two-day class, then a test. After just two weeks in Seattle, I'm sitting on a plane next to Ned, flying to Tokyo.

When we arrive, we board the bullet train to Fukuoka, a city on the southernmost of Japan's main islands. Pulling out of the train station, I see it in the distance—Mount Fuji, looking just as it did when I first saw it at six years old. I'm awestruck all over again by the huge mountain whose sides rise smoothly to meet a flat top covered by snow. Memories flash through my mind as I absorb its beauty and relish the recollections of sitting in the yard in reverence before this very sight.

The island we're headed to, Kyushu, is Japan's third largest. It's about 14,190 square miles and has two giant, active volcanoes that spew ash in whatever direction the wind blows. This ash often makes a mess of the homes—residents complain of having to shower off black ash several times a day. They often carry umbrellas to keep clean. Fukuoka, Kyushu island's biggest city, is on the northwest coast and is graced with expansive mountain views.

Within a week of arriving, Ned finds me a job teaching English for the Berlitz Language Center. I'm sent by bullet train to Osaka for a week of training. During that week, I realize that I seriously need to learn Japanese. Someone suggests I first learn to *read* the Japanese characters. *Really?* It sounds so incredibly difficult. But I decide to try.

At the Berlitz headquarters in Osaka, a lovely Japanese woman named Yuki helps me. Her English is good, and she teaches me the three alphabets in Japan.

"First came Kanji, about 2000 complicated characters, each one representing a word. They have been adapted from the Chinese written language.

"Second is Hiragana, which was developed to make sounding out Kanji easier. Each simple Hiragana symbol represents one sound. There are 46 sounds, so there are 46 Hiragana characters, one for each sound. The Hiragana characters 'live' under the Kanji characters everywhere, so it is easy to sound out Kanji.

"Third is Katakana. This alphabet is for all foreign words that make their way into Japanese, like *Macodonalado's* (which, of course, is what the Japanese call McDonald's). Like Hiragana, there is one Katakana character for each sound, so again, 46 total."

Yuki continues to guide me. "Study the Hiragana chart. Write it out each morning when you wake up and again at night before bed, and memorize the marks. Watch for the Hiragana characters under the Kanji."

I'm a quick study, and the pronunciation comes easily. Following her homework suggestion, I learn to write all the symbols within a week.

Now I can sound out and correctly pronounce Japanese, even though I don't know the meaning of the characters. But I'm diligent, and over the next three months I manage to learn the meanings of many characters. I even become confident having simple conversations in Japanese.

Although I've learned Japanese relatively quickly, I find teaching English to Japanese people much more difficult. English is so complicated. But I do my best, for four days every week.

One day, a Japanese friend tells me, "I read a report about literacy in America. It's amazing how many people cannot read in your country. We have one of the highest literacy rates in the world here. Why such a big difference?"

I don't know why English is so difficult, but this question reminds me of Jay. Why has he struggled so? He seemed always to be in trouble until he met Victoria, the girl who helped him make it through high school and college. *Was she his glasses to the world of reading?*

There are only a handful of foreigners this far south in Japan. Locals frequently stop me on the street or in stores. They ask me why I'm here.

One day a Japanese man asks if he can hire me as a helper to attend a beef convention in Osaka. He says that I will be given an outfit to wear and all I have to do is walk around being friendly. A week later, I board the bullet train.

When I arrive at the station in Osaka, I'm greeted by a polite Japanese man. He takes my suitcase, beckons me into a car, and drives me to a hotel next to the convention center. He escorts me to the lobby and hands me my suitcase, room key, and a large red bag. He bows and walks away.

The whole process is intriguing.

Once in my room, I empty the red bag. It's my outfit for the next five days: blue jeans, a Western-style blue top with snaps and a collar, a brown vest, cowboy boots, a red cowboy hat, a red bandana, and a sash like Miss America would wear that reads, "Miss Meat Fair." Indeed!

I have a grand old time greeting people at the convention and practicing my Japanese.

Every month or so, odd jobs like this spring up. At a business convention in Fukuoka, I dress up like a Playboy Bunny, along with several lovely Japanese women. We hand out little ice cream cones.

I also appear in several commercials. The first one is for a church by the sea that specializes in weddings. I wear a fancy dress and act like I'm one of the bride's guests; plus, I get to see a beautiful area of the Kyushu coast. Another commercial promotes a shopping mall. I wear an 18th-century lady's dress and an elaborate straw hat and hold a white parasol. I feel glamorous. Still another is for a "love hotel," where men go secretly to be with their concubines. For this I wear a red robe.

My last commercial is for fur coats. I stand next to a professional model who is serious and demure. In contrast, I feel pretty ridiculous—until it wraps and I'm handed the usual envelope, thick with yen.

Ned has been very attentive from the onset of this journey. In fact, I'm developing a pattern of falling into relationships. Nobody seemed to notice me when I was growing up, so now, when a man is benevolent toward me, when he shows attention, he effortlessly captures my heart. Ned is easy to talk to and kind. He always did entertain me with his wry humor and comical antics. I come to love his company, so we become a couple.

In our spare time, Ned and I explore the region together on our motorcycles. Once out of the city, the roads are smooth and winding, and we have them all to ourselves. We sometimes travel inland to the mountain areas where there are bamboo forests and rivers flowing through canyons. The countryside is covered with terraced rice fields and hot springs. We journey to the coast to see seaside villages, rugged beaches, more terraced rice fields, and hot springs.

One highlight is a resort that offers an opportunity to lie in a rectangular pit in the sand—a "sand coffin"—on the beach below the volcano Sakurajima. Each of us wearing a thin Japanese robe called a *yukata*, we're completely buried in extremely hot sand—only our heads protrude. Although supposedly healing, the sand burns my fanny.

We stay in bed-and-breakfast type places every night. They're called *ryokans*. They're easy to find in the Japanese travel booklet we have with us. One night we're deep in the mountains, far from any town, when it begins to get dark. Consulting our travel booklet, the closest *ryokan* is two hours away, but there is a "Love Hotel" close by. We decide to stay there.

Usually, people enter at the back of these Love Hotels, where a lit-up room chart above the private garage allows them to select their room. Once they make their choice, they're meant to enter the garage to hide their vehicle. An hourly rate is paid through a slot in the door before entering the room.

But Ned and I don't know this. We walk right in the front door, to the surprise of the innkeepers. The room they give us is spectacular. It's red, white, and pink, with a heart-shaped bed. A switch turns on a rotating light of many soft colors, a bit like in a disco.

The next morning, we wake up hungry. There is no food served at the Love Hotel, so we hop on our bikes and head for a nearby restaurant. We enjoy a typical Japanese breakfast of steamed local rice with a raw, farm-fresh egg cracked on top. The egg cooks as it is mixed with the hot rice. Strips of nori (dried seaweed) are dipped in soy sauce and laid on top. Then chopsticks are skillfully employed to wrap the rice mixture inside the nori, and I pop the delicious package into my mouth. Yum!

With the exception of the occasional Macodonalado's, every restaurant in Japan serves healthy, fresh, delicious food. Rice is served with nearly every meal. This moist, hot starch becomes one of my favorite foods.

Chapter 12

Festival of the Tooth

By 1987, I've been in Japan for three years and I'm ready for a change. Money is in the bank because of all the jobs in Japan, and I still have that travel bug.

I reluctantly say goodbye to Ned. He's been a wonderful companion, but I'm disappointed in myself. The dysfunction of my childhood seems to have crept into our relationship. Not only do I continue to allow myself to fall into relationships, I seem to let my temper get the better of me too often. It's frustrating—everything is business as usual until something upsets me. Instead of being calm and working through the problem, I get angry. I can't seem to figure out why. Suddenly, it's as though a mean woman has taken over and I hear myself yelling out of control. I don't like the person I become in those moments; it's almost like something inside me won't let me get too close to anyone.

Maybe I'm just supposed to be single. It sure is easier.

I take the "slow boat" to China on a large passenger ship. It's a relaxing three-day journey. In Shanghai, China's biggest city, I board a train that takes me to the center of the country. After a couple of weeks of touring, I take another train to Hong Kong.

Back to being solo, experiencing new landscapes and cultures, I'm feeling free and exhilarated again. Traveling alone is comfortable for me. I'm surprised when people ask, "Do you ever get lonely, anxious or scared?" Truthfully, to do whatever I want, whenever I want, is the ultimate freedom.

The Japanese saw the wisdom in the Kanji symbols the Chinese had been using for centuries, and I have learned them. So now, I'm able to communicate by writing. Speaking is a different beast. While Japanese is flat, lacking intonation, Chinese singsongs along from deep tones to high pitched. Everywhere I travel in China, I surprise the locals as an American woman who can communicate through writing.

One day, after a delicious meal of wonton soup in a tiny restaurant in downtown Hong Kong, I open my fortune cookie. "You long to see the pyramids in Egypt," the fortune says.

I notice a travel agency directly across the busy street. Finding a rare break in traffic, I quickly cross and enter the office. A friendly woman beckons me to take a seat in front of her desk. She shares an exciting itinerary: I can fly to Sri Lanka, spend 10 days, travel to Nairobi, Kenya for a three-week safari, and then take an open-ended layover in Egypt before landing in London.

"Sold!" I say to the woman. And with that, I'm off on my next adventure.

I wonder if the travel agency prints the fortune cookie messages.

Sri Lanka is an island nation south of India in the Indian Ocean. Its diverse terrain ranges from rainforest and arid plains to highlands and sandy beaches, with ancient Buddhist ruins nestled in along the way. From the airport, I hop a bus headed for a quaint resort right on the beach.

My view from the bus is an experience in itself. I am seeing life flash by in a blur of colors and people, some on bicycles, often two, three, or more people per bike. Elephants are everywhere. Men bathe the elephants in wide, murky rivers. Other men ride elephants that carry long logs with their trunks. Young boys climb coconut trees with ropes around their bare feet. The ropes keep their feet from separating more than about 16 inches, helping them climb the tall, smooth, branchless trunk.

The bus stops at a fruit stand, where whole bunches of bright yellow and green bananas hang by ropes. The fruit stand is a rundown shack.

A young man whacks the top off a coconut and I gulp down the sweet, cool liquid. When I've finished drinking, he chops the coconut in half. Eating the soft meat inside is a meal in itself.

That night at dinner, I sit down next to a young couple from India. They have come to see the "Festival of the Sacred Tooth." Excitedly, they explain, "It's a grand event that happens in the dark of night, with elegant costumes, cultural dances, fireball acrobats, and elephants adorned with lavish garments, all under a celebration of lights."

"What is the tooth?" I ask.

"It's the sacred tooth relic of Lord Buddha. Sri Lanka has been honored to house it in the Temple of the Tooth since the 16th century. This historical procession is held every year to pay it homage. You must join us!"

The next morning, we travel together in their rental car up into the mountains. By mid-afternoon, we arrive in a town called Kandy. There is much activity as the community prepares for this auspicious event.

When darkness falls, the music begins. Suddenly, dancers and drummers appear in the street. Everyone and everything is lit up with colorful lights. The crowd cheers. Then come dancers with flags, canopy bearers, whip crackers, spearmen and elephants, completely covered in bright fabrics with only their eyes showing. For three hours we watch the entertainment as jugglers, plate spinners, more than 40 elephants, more musicians, and endless dancers parade through the town.

The procession is magnificent, like nothing I've ever seen. Finally, a huge elephant adorned with a white-and-gold garment and red lights approaches. On its back is a tall, round housing with a pointed top and a red velvet pillow in the center. On the pillow sits the tooth. I can't see the tiny artifact, but my companions assure me it's there. It's a great honor to be so close to Lord Buddha's tooth.

Back at my beach *palapa*, the grass hut where I'm staying, I spend the days walking barefoot in the sand, enjoying the cool ocean breezes, reading and simply being in awe of my lush surroundings.

In the water, there are many tall poles with small seats fastened to them about halfway up. Men sit on these small seats, suspended over the ocean waves, a fishing pole in one hand and a net in the other.

At this small resort the dining area is a large, round room made of wood, with a grass roof like all the other structures. One night after dinner a band plays on the restaurant patio. I'm enjoying the music when I hear an accent I faintly recognize as northern European.

"Will you dance with me?" A strikingly handsome, blond-haired man with a warm smile is extending his hand.

"I'd love to," I say, looking over toward a table of several men laughing and winking at me.

"My friends," he says, and rolls his eyes.

We dance. I'm tingling with excitement. Dancing makes me feel free and alive. His ability to swing me around the small terrace surprises and delights me. When the band takes a break, he keeps hold of my hand and leads me off the deck toward the water. We walk down the beach.

When we can barely see the lights from the resort, he suggests we rest. We sit on a big log just beyond the reach of lapping waves.

His name is Bjorn, from Norway. He's a therapist who specializes in PTSD—post-traumatic stress disorder. He explains how fulfilled he feels by helping people recover from experiencing or witnessing a traumatic event.

"Tell me about yourself," he says, as he continues to look directly into my eyes.

I tell him about my time in Japan and my recent travels.

Suddenly, four or five Indian men jump out of the woods. They grab my arms and yank me to my feet. My heart races as I search the dark for Bjorn. As the native men wave large sticks in the air, I glimpse Bjorn running away down the beach.

Frantically, I fight. They have hold of my arms and legs, and are pulling me toward the woods. My sight is on the water as I battle to go toward it. They're jerking me away. I hear my shirt rip open. With all my might, I force us toward the water, knowing I cannot let them drag me into the woods.

Then one of the men, his dark skin close to my face, clamps his teeth down hard into my cheek. The instant pain takes all my attention and I feel them pulling me toward the woods.

Abruptly, they drop my body onto the sand. Bjorn is there with his friends, and they chase the men away.

I'm sobbing and shaking. Bjorn is holding me tightly and repeating the words, "They DID NOT succeed. You are safe."

Bjorn stays with me into the night. I cannot stop crying. He speaks in a gentle voice, reminding me over and over that they did not succeed, that I am safe. "Do not let your mind go to what might have happened. It didn't." His voice is soothing. "I know this was a traumatic event, I don't want to discount it. But I work with many people for whom things DID happen. Therapy and processing their feelings of fear and shame helps them. Let's pray for the people who need our understanding and compassion most."

Bjorn gives me his phone number. "We head home to Norway in the morning. Call me collect anytime, please. I'm so sorry this happened."

Finally, I'm calm enough to sleep.

Hunger pangs wake me sometime late in the day. I have a light meal of fresh fruit and then ask directions to find a phone. I call my father, collect.

"Are you okay?" I hear the concern in his voice. I tell him what happened and say I want to come home.

He listens, consoles me, and tells me to continue on my journey. "Get back in the saddle. Go to Africa. All will be well."

I am learning that horrible things happen in life, and no one gets away without one sort of tragedy or another. But sometimes the fear of what might happen or might have happened is greater than the event itself. I must also learn to trust the process of life.

Two days later, with a bruised soul and a bandaged cheek, I arrive in Nairobi, Kenya. Winding my way through dirt roads to the address I was given, I'm a bit apprehensive until I finally reach my fellow safari companions—16 travelers, plus the Kenyan driver, Kawame, and our tour guide, Abebe. Everyone seems to be around my age, 27, give or take. We're a mix of men and women, dark hair to light hair, big build to small. We're from Australia, Canada, Holland, England, Italy, and the Philippines. There's an instant closeness between us, 18 strong, that makes me feel comforted and excited for adventure all at once.

We throw our backpacks up on top of a huge old green African safari truck. It's a rugged vehicle that looks like it can take us anywhere.

"We go north, to Lake Turkana," says Abebe.

The first day is rough. Everyone must adjust to the terrible suspension as the truck bumps and knocks us all around, making its way up the rocky road. We crawl along at 25 miles per hour, but our pace seems to match that of Kenya's—no one seems to be in a rush to get anywhere.

We cover miles of grassland through a valley offering a magnificent view of Mount Kenya to the east. At last we reach a small game reserve where we settle for the night.

After we set up our tents, Abebe invites us to a local meal of rice and beans he's prepared. Children are playing up in the canopy of a dense acacia tree; they run around as though they are on solid ground. A herd of Masai giraffes walks off in the distance, and we're warned to watch out for baboons that may come into camp for handouts.

On the second day we head to Lake Nakuru, famous for its flamingos—one million at last count. They are beautiful as they strut around the shores of the lake, looking like pink cotton balls with long, thin legs and necks.

After dinner, we climb into the truck and go for our first game drive. We see impalas, water bucks, warthogs, baboons, hyenas, more varieties of birds than I've ever seen, and a roadrunner that looks straight out of a cartoon.

On the third day we cross the equator, all 16 of us crowding around the big sign for photos. By day five, we reach northern Kenya and Lake

Turkana. It's both the world's largest permanent desert lake and the world's largest alkaline lake. The rocky shores are home to scorpions, carpet vipers, and an abundance of Nile crocodiles.

The next day we are on the road again, traveling south in the big, bumpy old truck. We go from one national reserve to the next. The wildlife is phenomenal. Big herds of elephants, zebras, and flocks of ostriches are around every corner. We see a lion eating a fresh kill and hippopotamuses bathing in lakes. We drive by day and sleep in tents at night, except for in certain reserves where we stay in huts and lodges for safety.

We see many Kenyans walking along the roadside, women in brightly colored saris with huge baskets atop their heads and men who are naked except for a loincloth carrying long spears.

We stop in villages to fill up on supplies and meet the locals, some of whom are very curious about us. They approach cautiously for a closer look at my white face. The women of the Samburu tribe are striking, adorned with ornate headdresses and up to a hundred beaded neck-laces. Their faces are painted with elaborate orange designs. Some of the men have their hair completely covered with the same orange paint.

The third week we travel to what becomes my favorite place on the safari, Lamu. It's a town on Manda Island. It feels like a different world, a different century. We leave our truck and travel to Lamu by boat. There are no roads on the island, just alleyways and footpaths—very few motorized vehicles. Residents move about on foot or by boat; they use donkeys to transport goods and materials.

Walking through the narrow streets, I see many Islamic Arabians. The women are fully covered in black burkas, but for their eyes. Many of the men are in business suits, a sharp contrast to the Swahili Afri-cans whose necks and heads are covered in beads, who carry spears and barely wear a stitch of clothing.

Everyone is friendly, saying "Jambo," and smiling. On the first day in Lamu, as I walk through an alley with Pete from Holland, a Swahili man stops and talks with us. He's a fisherman and invites us to his home for fresh lobster and crab he has just caught. We follow the man and meet his wife and two small children at their hut on the outskirts of town. We have a delightful evening.

On the second day we all board a beautiful old sailing ship, called a *dhow*. The captain wears a T-shirt that says "Captain Hakuna Matata," Swahili for "No worries." We fish from the boat and swim in the warm, clear, turquoise water of the Indian Ocean. Looking back to the shore, I see beaches that stretch for miles, lined with palm trees. The spires on dozens of mosques rise up throughout the town.

After three days, we safari-goers are told it's time to pack up and head out. I want more time here, time to relax and enjoy this blended culture I find so fascinating. I feel this is a place I'll return to someday. I'll miss my companions, but I know it's time to move on.

My next stop is Egypt. After settling into a youth hostel in Giza, a small town on the other side of the Nile from Cairo, I'm amazed to see the pyramids are within walking distance.

I stroll along on this sunny, warm day through the bustling community. The pyramids grow large as I approach. The area is touristy, knickknack shops lining the road. I walk around and then go inside the Great Pyramid. A tour guide is telling a small group of tourists about harmonic alignment as I saunter through the King's Chamber. Suddenly, the guide is making tones, and the energy throughout my body feels alive and intense. There is a vibration in the room; it's otherworldly, surreal, as though this could be any time in the past, or the future. I can't make sense of it, but I like it.

Wandering around the Great Pyramid, I lose track of time. Eventually, I end up where I entered.

Atop a camel, I ride around the famous Sphinx. It's exhilarating to be in this dusty desert of legends and deep history. I want to stay longer, to ride a camel farther out with the sand under its hooves and a quiet oasis in my vision. I can't shake the feeling that something mystical happened to me in the King's Chamber. This is a special place.

Back at the youth hostel, I talk with a couple of young men who have just come from an adventure up the Nile River. Following their suggestion, I board a train headed to Aswan the next day. The 425-mile ride is scenic and takes me south along the Nile. That night, the rhythmic jostling of the train rocks me into a deep slumber in my sleeper car.

The next day, in Aswan, just as the two guys had promised, it's easy to find a group of young people putting a trip together. There are 16 of us. A man named Duncan, from London, who looks to be in his mid-20s, secures two *feluccas*, each with a captain and a cook.

The feluccas, the primary form of transportation on the Nile, are medium-sized sailboats, each with a flat deck through the middle where we lie around on blankets and soft cushions. Our backpacks are stored below. Traveling this way gives us the freedom to cruise between the great sites along the river, watching rural life pass us by. The Nile is much more beautiful and wider than I had expected, and the water looks clean. While the captain sails, our guide tells us about ancient Egypt.

At night, we all position ourselves around the felucca, cozy and warm with one blanket each and an article of clothing for a pillow. *The stars are magnificent*, I think as I drift off to sleep.

By the end of our four-day voyage, we have become a 16-member community, and together we decide to see more classic sights of Egypt. We land in Luxor, which is the home to two huge, ancient monuments that stand a mile apart—Graceful Luxor Temple and Karnak Temple. The royal tombs of the Valley of the Kings and the Valley of the Queens are on the river's west bank. We visit all the sites, taking local buses and touring the Valley of the Queens by donkey.

A huge excavation is happening at the Valley of the Kings. Two lead archaeologists in khaki clothing walk with intention from one deep hole in the ground to the next, up and down the dried mud steps. Egyptian workers haul buckets to and fro.

After three days of exploring the wonders, we head our separate ways. We exchange addresses and phone numbers and promise to stay in touch. Duncan and I board a bus bound for a small town on the coast of the Red Sea. We snorkel in the crystal-clear water and relax on the beach for a few days, then make our way back to Cairo. It's time for me to head home to America.

I'm glad my father made me continue my journey. I know that I'm searching for ways to learn, grow, and experience as much as I can in this life. Traveling opens my eyes to other ways of being in the world, offers new perspectives on how people go through their day, and awakens my sense of wonder.

Meeting people and learning who they are helps shape who I am in comparison. I eat new food and see new sights, absorbing the smells, tastes, beauty, hardship, joy, and pain, all at once. I feel more complete with each experience, having exchanged moments with these people in these places.

Sometimes meandering in foreign lands can be a challenge—overcoming language barriers, figuring out what to eat, where to sleep, and how to get to the next destination. Facing these struggles head-on and moving through to the other side has increased my self-esteem. Now, each time I arrive at a new place, I'm confident that within a few hours I'll be able to navigate around to the sites, find good food, and a place to sleep for the night. Everyday life seems a little easier. The unknown isn't as frightening. I know that I can tackle whatever comes my way.

Even with the attack on the beach, this journey has been a blessing—far more positive than negative. If something bad happens, I know that I'll learn, grow, and move through it, emerging on the other side as a richer, more whole citizen of the world.

Chapter 13

Titanic

From Egypt, I fly to San Diego to visit Jay, who is living his dream of working on films. He's been lucky to land a gig on *Titanic*. The director, James Cameron, has fired at least a dozen people from the accounting department. My brother is the only one who has been there since the beginning of the project.

Jay takes me to work with him the day after I arrive. At eight in the morning, we drive about an hour south across the U.S. border into Mexico. Forty-five minutes down the road, we round a corner and there is the massive ship in the water just offshore, near the town of Rosarito. It's leaning at a 30-degree angle and looks like it's sinking, but in fact it's being held in place by an enormous steel structure that's hidden on the ocean side of the ship.

As we get closer, I see people all around the ship's decks. I exclaim in confusion, "What?"

Jay is laughing. "They're just dummies!"

Jay gets a special pass for me. While he works in the makeshift office building, I tour around the ship and the grounds all day. I'm completely spellbound by the fine details of the ship, inside and out. On the shore sits a huge building that houses the sets for the underwater scenes. It's amazing to observe some of the filming.

While I stroll, I think about Jay and our interactions over the years. I remember being afraid of him growing up, but things shifted after the trip to Southern California with my boyfriend, Dan. We're now able to have open, from-the-heart conversations. We've taken some trips together, to see family on the East Coast and a vacation to the Virgin Islands for spring break when I was in college. We talk on the phone often. I love the person Jay is, the person he's become. He's one of my best friends.

Later, at dinner, I can't help but notice that he has a couple of beers.

"I'm happy enough here," he tells me. "The work is okay, but I'd rather be closer to the cameras. Being a cameraman is a dream beyond my reach. Cameramen need to know how to read."

Letters confuse him, but numbers are easy. "Numbers play fair, they're consistent," he says.

"So, did your high school girlfriend, Victoria, help you get through high school and college?" I ask.

"I wouldn't have graduated from high school or gotten into college without her," says Jay.

I nod, though I'm surprised. I had no idea her support had run so deep.

"There's a girl here who helps me," Jay continues. "She's in public relations and has a son who can't read. He's in trouble with the law." Like Jay, he didn't have a care in the world until grade school, when the reading monster appeared and changed everything.

"I'm so sorry, Jay."

"Why? I'm just dumb."

I don't know what to say to assure him that I know he's not "dumb."

Jay changes the subject by asking, "What's next for you?"

"Well, I'm 27 years old. There's plenty of money in my savings account. What do I want to do next? That's what I need to figure out."

"The world is open for people who can read, Narda," he says. "You can do anything."

Chapter 14

Idaho

After a week of being in Southern California with Jay, I head back to Seattle. It's early January. I want to go someplace away from the bleak rain and cold, but not too far away this time. Being a ski bum for the winter seems like a fun idea. Dad loves to ski and he made sure we skied almost everywhere we lived, even in Japan. I started skiing when I was four years old at Crystal Mountain when we lived in Tacoma, Washington.

I remember meeting a guy in Seattle a few years back. Martin Marley was his name, and he lived in Idaho. He was a ski instructor in Sun Valley through the winter and a fly-fishing guide in the summer.

I give Martin a call. "I'm thinking of spending the winter in Sun Valley. Will you be around?"

"Sure," he says. "Come on out. The skiing is great. You can stay on my couch until you find your own place."

After a few more days of seeing family and friends, I pack my bags, say goodbye to drizzly Seattle and am on the road to Idaho. It's an easy 11-hour drive on a four-lane highway over the Cascade mountains, through the open vistas of southeastern Washington, over the Blue Mountain range in central Oregon, and finally crossing the border into Idaho.

Within 30 miles of Sun Valley, snow begins to appear on the sides of the road. As I drive north on Highway 75, the snowbanks grow higher and so does my excitement. Entering the small town of Ketchum, I realize I'm in a full-on winter wonderland. The glistening snow and crisp air are a far cry from where I started my journey.

Martin is an ideal host for a few days. I find a condo to rent in Ketchum, a one-mile drive to the ski lifts. I buy a ski pass and spend my days on the mountain. More than once I think, *How did I get so lucky?*

I keep seeing a tall, thin man around town—in the lodge when I take a break for cocoa, speeding by on the slope, clicking his ski poles. He often jumps on the chairlift with me and other skiers. He stands out with his brilliant blue eyes, darkly tanned skin, bright blond hair and mustache. He also has a long, thin, braided ponytail down his back. My type? *I think not.*

One night in town, I reach out to open the door to a restaurant and there he is again.

"I see you everywhere," I say.

"That's because I'm following you," he replies with a wink.

I turn to join my girlfriends.

The next day he jumps on the chairlift with me. We chat about the good skiing and the quaint town of Ketchum. Just before we off-load, he asks, "How about meeting me tonight in town?"

"I've got a date," I reply. I actually do have a date—it's not a lame excuse. "But if it goes south, I'll stop by the Sawtooth Club afterwards."

Later that evening, after my planned, mediocre date heads home, I enter the Sawtooth Club. He's on the couch by the fireplace with a drink in his hand. He's alone. I order a drink at the bar, then make my way over to the couch.

Sitting down next to him, I ask, "What's your name again?"

"Eric," he says. Then he asks, "How was your date?"

"Just okay," I say with a shrug. "Thought I'd have a nightcap."

We start chatting. Eric tells me about his years growing up in a suburb just outside New York City. He says school never really engaged him. Prep school was too easy and boring. He wasn't interested in going to college. With no idea what he wanted to study, liberal arts classes had no appeal. All he wanted to do was ski. His parents took him to the Port Authority in New York City and put him on a bus bound for Idaho when he was 17 years old, thinking he would come running home within the year.

"That was 15 years ago," he says.

He loves his life. He's a construction worker during the summer and is a full-on ski bum in the winter. He's making me laugh and feel at ease. *This guy is witty and cute. Maybe he'd like to be my boyfriend for the winter. Would he?*

Eric and I ski together every day. After a couple of weeks following him around the mountain, I can imitate his unique style of skiing. It's exhilarating when we ski side by side, making the exact same short, rapid moves. As we make our tightly carved turns, our upper bodies are still while our legs are in an extremely angular position. We ski close together, in precise unison. We get cheers from skiers on the chairlift above us.

When the mountain closes in the spring, I feel it's time for me to move on with my life. I've done the ski bum thing and it was terrific.

Eric pleads with me, though. "Please stay. If you've never tried mountain biking, you'll be amazed, I guarantee it." In no time, he's convinced me to stay for the summer.

As the saying goes in Sun Valley, "the winters will bring you, but the summers will keep you." I find that out for myself, and Eric's right—mountain biking becomes my new passion. It's like hiking through the woods, except on a rugged bike that can climb up a hill over rocks and tree roots and then whiz down the other side through endless nature trails. I'm hooked—not just on this newfound sport but also on this quaint mountain town. And on Eric. I have fallen in love. I find myself moving into Eric's charming home—we've been together five months.

But I need a job. There are few options in this small ski town: I can work for Sun Valley Company or get a job in retail or in real estate. I choose real estate because helping people find a home sounds like fun; it sounds meaningful. After just one week of real estate classes, I pass the test. It's enjoyable touring people through beautiful homes, watching their expressions as they find their perfect match or imagine their future selves calling these walls their home. With my strong organizational skills, nothing slips through the cracks. I steadfastly hold clients' hands through the expensive, often-stressful process. My reputation as a solid, hard-working agent builds and my business thrives.

A couple of years into our relationship, Eric raises the idea of getting married.

I've already thought about this.

I say, "Let me list your house. Let's buy land and build a home. If we can make it through building a home together, let's get married!"

When we are halfway through building our home, Eric gets down on one knee in the living room—the floors are still plywood—and proposes. I say yes, and we go to town for dinner. Tom Nickel, the proprietor of the Sawtooth Club restaurant where we had our first date by the fireplace, sends a bottle of champagne to our table.

I'm happy and excited about this next phase of my life. Eric has the bluest eyes; they look at me with sincerity. Though we've had some ups and downs, I trust myself to be a good partner to this wonderful man in this lovely quiet town.

In the fall of 1991, we get married at the Idaho Rocky Mountain Ranch in the Sawtooth Valley, about an hour north of Ketchum. We spend our honeymoon driving a tiny, four-wheeled vehicle around Kyushu, Japan, to places I traveled long ago by motorcycle. I want Eric to experience and delight in some of the people and places I remember so well.

While in Japan we stop in to see Ned, who is happily married to a kind Japanese woman. How comforting to see my old friend so content.

The spring after Eric and I marry, we want to start a family. In preparation for getting pregnant, I give up alcohol and sugar to create the best possible temple for our growing baby. My mother drank while pregnant with me—she didn't think about the effect it might have on my brain.

I'm pregnant within months. In February of 1993, I give birth to our daughter, Sadieanne, whom we affectionately call Sadie. She is beautiful and joyful.

Inevitably, life changes. It feels so abrupt. Eric continues to work while I take some time off to care for the baby. But my phone keeps ringing and clients need me. I don't want to tell them to go elsewhere, so I bring Sadie with me, everywhere. Life gets complicated as I juggle a baby and clients, feedings, diapers, and interrupted sleep with showings, offers and endless paperwork.

I become agitated and can't help but feel Eric is not helping me enough. I get angry, and that mean woman takes over my body, yelling out of control.

I'm pregnant again when Sadie is about three months old.

Later that year, the holidays hit like a ton of bricks, toppling over me. I'm overwhelmed and frazzled. I go to a therapist who brings up my alcoholic mother's behavior during my childhood.

The therapist mentions that one reason the holidays are such a challenge for people is that alcohol is typically flowing and emotions run high. She suggests that my chaotic state of mind is rooted in my experience as a child during family celebrations, when my mother had to calm her nerves by drinking.

Okay, this is making sense, let's just get through the holidays.

Two weeks after Sadie has her first birthday, I give birth to our son Raleigh.

Having two little babies is hard, and I feel off balance a lot of the time. While before children and marriage I was as free as a bird, now I'm tethered to daily responsibilities, to other beings who constantly need my focus and attention.

My relationship with Eric is deteriorating. We disagree on how to discipline our children. Maybe this is because Eric's childhood had strict boundaries, whereas mine was marked by total freedom and chaos. We both have full-time jobs, and argue over who should do the ever-growing number of chores.

I search for that peaceful place in my mind, but it is nowhere to be found.

Chapter 15

Prison

The spring that Sadie is born, Jay calls me. He's met a nice girl named Jenny.

"I'm in love with her," he says. "I love her company. She's easy to talk to." He goes on to describe her pretty, long blonde hair and kind hazel eyes. She has two older children from a previous marriage, Jeremy and Jessica. Jay says they're polite, adorable kids who get good grades. The good grades really impress him. "All of our names begin with 'J,' he says. "It's meant to be!"

A few months later, he calls again. "Jenny's pregnant."

Jay moves in with Jenny full time to make a go of their relationship. They live in a nice apartment in San Clemente, California, with a view of the ocean.

When I speak with Jay, he seems to be holding it together fairly well. I am pregnant with my second child, so Jenny and I become close, sharing the grievances and delights of pregnancy.

The following February, Jenny gives birth to AJ. Three weeks later, Raleigh is born.

For the next three years, between 1994 and 1997, Jay and I travel back and forth between California and Idaho, visiting each other and tightening the bond between our families. Our kids play together and we play with them. I feel happy during these times, but I see that Jay is struggling. He's still working on *Titanic*, and things are heating up. James Cameron is taking more time than anyone expected, and the spending is out of control. On top of that, there are more firings in the accounting department. Jay is under constant stress.

One early evening on his way home from work in Mexico, Jay gets pulled over just inside the U.S. border. He's charged with driving under the influence—DUI. A couple of weeks later, again returning from work, Jay is pulled over a second time. It's late in the evening. He gets his second DUI. Less than a week later, he's stopped again—his third DUI. This time, he's hauled off to jail.

Having made bail a few days later, Jay is sitting in his living room, completely broken in spirit. He contemplates his drinking. "I'm scum. Lock me up," he says. And that they do. For seven months.

Shortly after Jay goes to prison, the film finally wraps. My brother's name appears in the credits of *Titanic:* "Accounting—Albert (Jay) Pitkethly."

The prison is in the desert east of L.A. It's a rough group of men, so Jay keeps to himself. He feels lonely, and he desperately misses AJ. Being someone who likes to stay busy working, Jay is bored. The food is absolutely awful—barely edible. He is totally miserable and frantic for a way out. He hears that a transfer to the nearby prison, which has an infirmary, often leads to an earlier release. So, Jay feigns a back injury, saying he can't move from his cot. The warden doesn't believe him and throws him into solitary confinement for two weeks. It's a cold, cramped, pitch-black cement room.

My heart breaks for Jay, knowing how alone and scared he must be. He's made mistakes, but my brother has revealed himself to be a good man. He's shed the cruelty and bullying of his childhood years, which I suspect was always a cover for his deep insecurities, but now alcohol has become that mask yet again. Like a demon waiting in the wings, it's always ready to strike whenever his defenses are down.

Later, Jay tells me he'd rather be dead than in that frightening place ever again. The hours and days dragged on. He believed he was losing his mind.

When Jay is finally released, he calls me. His voice is trembling. "I *must* stop drinking, Narda. If I mess up, next time they'll lock me up for a lot longer. I can't go back. Please, can I come to Sun Valley? I'll be safe there with you."

"Yes!" I answer, without hesitation.

I'm thrilled when Jay comes to Sun Valley in 1998. He buys a condo down the street from me and lands a job with a recruiting company. AJ is five years old, and Jenny says that he can move to Sun Valley to live with Jay for a while. Jay and Jenny split up, but stay friends. AJ goes to elementary school with Raleigh and Sadie.

Jay and AJ become the delight of the town. They look alike. Jay is handsome, with big, brown eyes and dark, wavy hair; AJ is his "mini-me." Often, they wear identical shirts. With their father–son comic performances—reciting lines from funny movies, bantering delightfully back and forth, making funny faces in tandem or singing a song together, Jay baritone and AJ high-pitched—they leave a trail of laughter behind them everywhere they go.

The 12-step recovery community embraces Jay. Gradually, I can see the sparkle return to my brother's eyes. I'm so relieved. Life feels fresh and new. Jay and I are happy to be near each other. We go camping on the weekends just north of town. We all love being by the creek, in the woods, in the still calm air. In the summer, Jay, AJ, Sadie, and Raleigh ride BMX bikes. I even jump on a bike and race sometimes, though cheering from the sidelines is more my speed. Racing bikes around a dirt track is competitive, and I don't like competing.

Out on a hike one day, little AJ has to go number two. As a Southern California boy, he's not accustomed to pooping in the woods and is on the brink of tears. "Okay AJ," his dad says. "Lie on the ground. Narda and Sadie—take his left leg; Raleigh and I will take his right. On the count of three, lift him into the air. One, two, three LIFT!"

Amidst loving laughter, we hold AJ's little six-year-old body upside down. "How's it now, AJ?" Jay asks.

"It's working! I don't need to poop anymore!" AJ replies.

Jay tells me often that AJ is the best thing that has ever happened to him. "With all the struggles in my life, I've wanted to die. Now, I'm so happy to be alive because I get to share my life with my son. AJ is my partner, my main dude, the love of my life."

Jay's biggest frustration is that AJ is a struggling reader; like his dad, he hates school and refuses to do his homework.

Sadie has difficulty reading, too. One day, in first grade, her teacher calls Eric and me in to tell us that Sadie will be pulled out of class for 30 minutes every day to work with the school's reading specialist.

I'm glad that Sadie is getting the help she needs. But I'm also confused. *How could I learn to read Japanese in a week, while Sadie, and now AJ, struggle to read their own language?* I know something is profoundly wrong with this picture.

I start researching.

To my shock, I learn that—according to the National Institute of Child Health and Human Development—*one in four* children born and raised in America grows up not knowing how to read. And according to the U.S. Department of Education, 19 percent of high school students in America graduate unable to read above a third-grade level, which is considered *functionally illiterate.* That's nearly one in five students, or half a million new graduates each year! How can that be?

I also learn that a huge percentage of challenged readers end up in prison. The National Assessment of Adult Literacy reports that, in America, 85 percent of juvenile delinquents and 70 percent of prison inmates are functionally illiterate. I realize that these statistics describe Jay—both his challenges with reading and his time in prison.

Something clicks. I'm beginning to understand Jay in a way I haven't before. These are national statistics, and the implications are very, very personal. I begin thinking seriously about how to help people learn to read.

Chapter 16

Raleigh

Raleigh has not always been one to do the right thing. The day he learns to crawl, he takes one of Sadie's tidily organized shoes in his mouth, crawls across the room and places it into the dirt of a houseplant. A few minutes later, when Sadie discovers her shoe in the soil, she has a complete meltdown. Raleigh sits nearby, laughing so hard that his arms are flailing.

At every opportunity, he distresses his older sister.

He also torments his father and me. Putting Raleigh to bed is the worst. Every evening it's the same routine. At the end of a long day, I'm tired, but not Raleigh. He jumps up and down in his crib until all hours of the night, and then he's awake before everyone, banging his toys against the wall.

Once he can talk, every night he commands, "I want to play! Read me another story! Rub my feet again! Rub my back, my legs, my arms, my hands!"

One night in particular, Raleigh is giving me his usual fuss about not wanting to go to sleep. Eyeing the open window across from his crib, I seriously consider tossing him out of it. But then I remember that my thoughts are like passing clouds—I can choose to act on them, or let them float along.

When Raleigh is old enough to tell time, I trick him by moving all the clocks in the house an hour ahead. "Look how late it is. You want to be fresh for school in the morning." It works!

Whether because of the added stress of kids, the mean woman who sometimes takes over, or just the natural way people sometimes drift apart, when the kids are just four and five years old, Eric and I realize that, truthfully, we have fallen out of love. We decide to stop exposing our children to the constant bickering and, hopefully, to the crazy woman that takes over my mind. We read up on how to have the best divorce. Books like *Mom's House, Dad's House* say that the best thing we can do is to live close to each other. If the kids can easily get to Mom's house from Dad's, and vice versa, that would be the best situation for them.

We see a therapist to make sure we're doing the best we can for our children in this difficult situation. Then we sell the wonderful house we built together, where Eric proposed and where our children have grown, and each of us purchases a new home. It's like losing a limb, but I know it's the right decision. The two homes are about a mile apart, with the elementary school in between. Sadie and Raleigh go from one house to the other every Friday.

During our separation, moving into our separate homes and for a few months beyond, Eric and I have an emotional, often mean-spirited divorce. We're fighting over money and who gets what.

Even after we give up the fight, it takes a year of consistent determination to recover our friendship. Eric is making an effort. When he has the kids, he often calls in the evening—Sadie and Raleigh want to say goodnight. Sometimes, when the kids are with him, he invites me over to eat, play a game or go for a walk so we can be all together like a family.

Slowly, I come around and return Eric's thoughtfulness. One act of reciprocated kindness after another, we build a new kind of friendship. He ends up becoming one of my best friends. I can talk with him anytime about my troubles; he understands me more deeply than anyone. Sometimes it feels like Eric knows me better than I know myself. I'll call in a panic about someone I'm seeing, and tell him that the witch has taken over my body. "Remember, when you overreact, it's something from childhood," he'll say. "Get some rest and some exercise. Call me anytime."

On the first day of preschool, Raleigh finds a new focus for his attention. He loves to learn. His preschool teacher is a bright, young woman named Kristin Mayle. She pulls me aside one day. "Would it be okay if I tried something with Raleigh in math?"

Kristin teaches Raleigh his times tables. *Is this normal at his age? In preschool?*

Raleigh is not only great at math, he's a good reader, too. I'm overcome with relief.

The next year, when Raleigh starts kindergarten at Hemingway Elementary, he hits a wall. He comes home from his first day and says, "Mom, guess what we learned in school today? To count to twenty."

For a boy who already knows his times tables, learning to count hardly holds his interest. Boredom soon turns to disruption. Eric and I are at a loss. Our answer comes two weeks later, when Raleigh is kicked out of kindergarten.

Good, now we can hopefully move Raleigh to a place that challenges him.

We're grateful that the Pioneer Montessori School in Ketchum is willing to take him for the rest of the year.

In first grade, he returns to Hemingway with the best teacher ever, Ms. Char Roth. Raleigh wakes up early every morning, eager for the day. "Mom, can we leave yet?" he chants as he emerges from his bedroom.

I'm not a bad mom. My body clock says to wake up at 7 a.m., leaving an hour and a half to get the kids dressed, fed, and ready, with lunches in their backpacks and time to walk to school by 8:30. It seems reasonable. But some mornings, when I wake, I find Raleigh already gone. *That darn kid escaped again. But I know where he went—three blocks away to school!*

I soon receive a call from the principal. "You need to keep Raleigh home until school starts. The janitor found him before 7 a.m. this morning sitting on the lobby floor, reading."

Though Raleigh loves being at school, he's a bit of a loner, comfortable at home with his toys, playing with balls of every sort, enjoying our pets. We have cats, a dog, and a bunny. At Eric's place, there are many tanks filled with fish, turtles, and snakes. An entire room is dedicated to iguanas.

When Raleigh is 10, we send him to camp—hiking, mountain biking, horseback riding, archery, and swimming in frigid mountain lakes. Eric drops him off 30 miles north of Ketchum in the Boulder Mountains.

At 10 p.m. that night, Eric gets a call. "Raleigh is here in the office, packed and ready to go home. Please come pick him up."

"What's the problem?" Eric demands.

"Well, at orientation, after dinner, one of our counselors shared our rules and precautions for wilderness living—that deer mice live around the cabins and sometimes get inside. He explained that their droppings are poisonous. Some of the boys scared Raleigh, saying the poisonous poop was under his bed. Now he wants to go home."

Eric brings him home. So much for camp.

I see myself in Raleigh—the withdrawn, antisocial Narda from childhood. After some reflection, I realize that my solitude is born from shame and fear, whereas Raleigh's is simply because he is comfortable with himself.

Chapter 17

A Married Sandwich

In 1998, Raleigh is five years old and Sadie is six. I haven't been back to Seattle to visit my family in over six months. I decide to drive over solo, during Eric's week with the kids.

When I walk into Mom's kitchen in Kirkland, Washington, Walter VanWinkle is standing there. He's holding an empty glass, milk mustache on his upper lip. Wavy black hair sticks out at all angles as he turns to see who's walked in. His green eyes are striking. His trousers are too big, and are held up on his thin frame by an old, grey leather belt. He's 12 years younger than Mom, and despite the eccentricities, he's distractingly handsome.

Mom enters the kitchen. "Oh Narda, I'm so happy you're here!" She gives me a long hug. "I see you've met Walter."

He looks like a giant next to my petite mom.

Walter reaches out for her and pulls her to him. She giggles. I have never heard this delightful sound from my mother before. She's looking at him with complete adoration. I'm floored.

Mom beckons to me. "Come see the studio. I want to show you the new glassblowing tools Walter built." I can feel a loving energy flowing between her and Walter as we walk out the front door.

Walter is a welder and a craftsman. First, Mom shows me all the clever new parts he's constructed for the studio—many specialized tools and tables. We then head to the garage, where the rusted body of a 1950 Chevy truck is up on blocks. Walter is restoring it into a functioning vehicle.

"You'll be riding in it within a year," says Mom. Walter plans on rebuilding the engine, painting the body a light purple, and entering it as the Kirkland Arts Center's float in the annual Fourth of July parade.

"And look what Walter's done with the pool," Mom says, as she takes my hand and leads me out behind the house, continuing our Walter show-and-tell, with Walter following right behind. The pool sparkles. No leaves floating or dirt around the drain. "I'm in the pool all the time now," Mom says.

I notice her skin is glowing with a healthy tan.

"Let's swim," Walter says. He's a man of few words and a big smile.

"I'll get my swimsuit," I say eagerly, walking back toward my car. Collecting my suitcase, I walk into the house and go down the stairs to the ground-level basement. This became my room when brother Dave went off to college. It has long, rectangular windows at the top of the far wall. Through the glass, I can see the earth underneath the rose garden.

The room always made me feel grounded and far away from the family chaos. Opening my suitcase on the floor in the corner, I recall my early teenage years when Mom clomped around above me in the kitchen all night long. "I'm on patrol," she used to say. She would sleep by day and be up all night, drinking.

Now, the room seems less gloomy. I hear laughter coming from above.

As I make my way back upstairs, I realize how everything feels clean. The air is fresh. Stepping outside, my bare feet feel good on the tiles that are warmed by the sun. The water in the pool is sparkling and delightfully cool, but not cold. It's inviting.

I swim over to Mom, who is lounging on a float shaped like an alligator. Treading water, I say, "I've never seen the pool look so good. Where did you meet Walter?"

"We met at a recovery meeting."

"Do you still go to meetings?"

"Yes, our favorite group is on Friday nights, in downtown Kirkland. Narda, I've never felt so happy."

Suddenly, a shadow covers us. We look up to see a large figure on the roof.

"Oh no! Watch out!" cries Mom. We quickly swim toward the shallow end. The next thing I know, there's an enormous splash in the deep end. Walt has jumped off the roof.

After dinner, he disappears into the garage to work on his Chevy, while Mom and I take a walk around the neighborhood. We pick up large rocks from the side of the road to carry along with us, which keeps our arms strong for glassblowing.

"Walter is an odd duck, Narda. He grew up poor and never went to college. He's bright, but simple. His father was an alcoholic and very abusive." Mom proceeds to tell me how Walter had a bedwetting problem as a kid. Each morning his dad would grab him by the hair and drag him out of bed. If the sheets were soiled, Walter was thrown into a freezing cold shower while his father stood outside the curtain, counting the minutes.

"Wow, that's mean." I think about how hard that would have been for Mom's new friend.

"Walter seems nice enough," I say. "He sure adores you."

"You know that your father and I got stuck together when I was 19 and he was 20. I was pregnant, and back then people got married if a baby was on the way. My dream was to be a doctor. My mom was a nurse, my father was a doctor and all my siblings became physicians. Your father got to be a neurosurgeon. My dream was ruined when, all of the sudden, I was having a baby."

"I know."

"I'm sorry for spoiling your childhood. I wish I could go back and do it differently."

"It's okay, Mom. Mostly, I just felt alone. It made me independent."

"I kept having babies, thinking more kids would make me happy." Alcohol calmed her nerves and made it easier when she had to join our father for physicians' events. "I started waking up needing, wanting alcohol. Reality slipped away. Support from 12-step recovery members was the only thing that kept me sober."

"Do you love Walter?"

"I love being put on a pedestal for the first time in my life. Walter does so much around here. He's grateful that he doesn't have to work a nine-to-five job. He's learning to blow glass. I love that together we don't drink. Did you notice I've stopped smoking?"

The next day, Mom and I get up early to blow glass. My brother Richard stops by to blow glass with us. We trade off assisting one another. It's the best day ever.

As I relax that afternoon and wander around the house, I notice sticky notes everywhere. They are rough, handwritten notes, saying, "I love you on a lazy Wednesday," "Hi again, one note just wasn't enough. I spent most of the day thinking about you and how wonderful it is with you," and "Hi Susan, I love you. It feels like a dream it's so good. I'm glad it's real. I love you."

Mom's strength grows in her words and actions. Her glass art blossoms into magnificent, unique pieces. She publishes a website for The Glass Kingdom. Her phone rings off the hook with orders from galleries all over the world. She's commissioned to make an ornament for the White House Christmas tree. She and Walter go to many fundraisers, mostly in the Seattle area. Mom donates her art to various causes; her pieces are frequently in live auctions and sell for thousands of dollars.

I watch with gratitude as my mother's life unfolds into this new place of artistic expression, healthy habits and a gentle, kind man who loves her so fully. Would she have been this content as a doctor? Maybe, but maybe not. That might have been one dream. But now she is realizing a dream she never knew she had.

Soon, Mom becomes involved with the local Ikebana Club, reviving her interest in the ancient Japanese art of flower arranging that she learned when we lived in Japan. All the women attending are Japanese. Most don't speak English—only Japanese—which jogs Mom's memory of the language. Ikebana in glass becomes her new artistic inspiration. Her pieces are phenomenal, delicate and beautiful.

One winter morning, my phone rings. It's Mom. "Hi, Narda. Come for another visit. Why don't you fly over with the kids this time? Walter and I will drive you back to Sun Valley. Walter wants to learn to ski."

And that's what we do, fly to Seattle for a delightful week with Grandma and Walter.

On the 700-mile drive back to Idaho together, I'm amazed to think about this woman who was a stranger in my childhood, but now is a compassionate grandmother and my best confidante.

Walter often asks Mom to marry him. His entreaties are met with giggles and, "Oh Walter, you're sweet."

One day Mom calls with a new idea. "I've stepped down as president of the Kirkland Arts Center. But this year I'm heading up fundraising and have a fantastic fundraising idea. Walter and I will get married at the Kirkland Arts Center next Valentine's Day, and we'll ask for donations in lieu of wedding gifts. All the artists want to help and everyone in town will be invited. Isn't this all such fun?"

"I love it!"

My brother Richard helps, and we get to work crafting glass-blown mini "Glass Kingdoms" to give out to everyone who attends the wedding.

The wedding itself is enchanting. Mom's artist friends do most of the work—the decorations, the food, the flowers, and the music. Walter surprises everyone by arriving with a dazzling, artistic wedding cake. Bubbles are blown instead of rice being thrown. At Walter's request, he and Mom honeymoon at Disney World. It's Walter's first visit there, and they have a delightful time.

The next visit to Mom's is as entertaining as ever. Walter and the kids play for hours in the pool, while Mom, Richard, and I blow glass. Walter comes into the studio every day and says, "It's time for a lunch break. Susan, I've made you a married sandwich!"

Mom rolls her eyes and laughs. "What have you made today, Walter?"

Each married sandwich is something crazy, like carrots and whipped cream. "Oh well, he's awfully cute, don't you think?" she says to me. He is indeed.

Chapter 18

Back at the Gateway

One day during the newly-married bliss that is Mom's and Walter's world, Jay stops by my house to talk.

"I want to meet a nice woman and fall in love," he tells me. "I've been single since Jenny and I broke up—a long time. The problem is … I'm too shy. With a little drink, though, I loosen up."

Then he tells me that Chandler's restaurant has hired him to bartend three nights a week. Seeing the concern in my expression, he says, "Don't worry, Narda. If I have a drink after work, I'll mix it really weak. You know—cocaine was my problem, not alcohol."

"You promise to make your drinks weak?" I ask, naively.

In my ignorance, I don't see that even a weak drink will lead Jay back to drugs, in the same way that drugs lead back to alcohol. It's a destructive path that is always beckoning.

Suddenly, Jay and I don't talk every day as usual. It's a busy time in real estate and I'm distracted. I don't notice.

Three weeks slip by. Then Jay is gone and my life is changed forever.

I'm dreaming. The search for Jay continues, in the woods. Jay steps out from behind a tree and takes my hands in his. He looks into my eyes and says, "Narda, we planned this long ago, before we were born onto this earth. It's going to be okay, it has to be this way. Trust me."

I wake up to grass tickling my cheek. I'm disoriented. I'm on the bank of the Big Wood River, my legs sweaty in my hot waders. *Oh, I'm searching again.*

It's late afternoon by the time I get to Hailey and plod out of the river. My legs are shaking with fatigue. I collapse into the first car that stops for me.

The driver asks, "Where's your fishing pole?"

"It's a long story," I say.

He drops me back at my car in Gimlet, six miles up the road. I barely have the energy to drive home.

By day, everywhere I go, I am searching. By night, in my dreams, I am searching.

One night, I dream I'm in a forest thick with trees. I see a clearing up ahead. As the trees thin and I walk into the opening, I see Jay's body strapped to a grid made of sticks and logs. His face is half gone. Large chunks are gouged out of his exposed legs and arms. I awaken in a cold sweat, crying and gasping for air.

Every time I arrive at the door of my home, I stop. As if I can will my brother to appear, I pray; *Please, Jay, be on my couch. Show me your familiar grin that says, 'Sorry, I messed up. I'll make you laugh and you'll forgive me.'*

On October 31, after 44 days of searching, snow falls. I'm exhausted and can't get out of bed. I lie there feeling like someone has kicked me in the stomach. I feel like I'm melting away into oblivion, like Jay.

Friends stop by with food. I eat little. I want to disappear. My children—Sadie, eight years old, and Raleigh, seven—have been staying with their dad for weeks. When the searches began, Jenny took AJ to a place near Seattle not far from Mom.

So not only are Jay's whereabouts a total mystery, AJ is suddenly gone from my life, too. There's a huge hole in my heart, and my soul feels like it is leaking downstream, slipping away.

In the late afternoon, I hear a knock at my front door, and then, "Mom?"

"I'm in bed," I call weakly, down the stairwell.

I hear light thumping as two sets of feet run up the carpeted stairs. Suddenly, my children are standing next to my bed.

"We want to come home, Mom. We love being at Dad's, but we miss you. We miss Uncle Jay. We miss AJ. When do we get our happy Mommy back?"

I've missed them, too.

My children climb onto the bed and rub my feet as I sob. Wads of tissues dot the floor.

That evening, in my hopeless state, I focus on my mission to find Jay. Any result short of this goal is unacceptable. My fingers press against my temples. *Think! Think! We didn't find his body. He must be alive.*

Dad

Jay shaking hands with President Johnson

Narda's passport photo 1970

Christmas in Japan. Back row: Jay and Dave
Front row: Richard, Narda, and Tom

Pits Pita Pat

Family photo. Back row: Dave, Dad, Mom
and Jay. Front row: Richard, Taiho,
Narda, and Tom

Miss Meat Fair

BMX: Jay, AJ, Raleigh, and Sadieanne

AJ and Jay

Mom and Jay
(Jay's college graduation)

Richard

Search area

Sadieanne, Eric, Raleigh, and Narda

Susan's degree in chemistry and her training certification in the Sogetsu School of Japanese flower arranging has led to originating glass plant material to combine with containers and goblets. These works are an intricate sculptural form. Their sinuous lines relate closely to their organic origins, and each of the flower-bearing plants offers a new and unique design.

PARTIAL LIST OF EXHIBITS ◆ AWARDS ◆ GALLERIES

2003 — Permanent display in new Environmental Protection Agency (EPA) building, Washington, D.C.

April 1999 — "Passions Afire," Pilchuck Glass School, City Center, Seattle, Wash.

June 1998 — "Patterns" two-person show, Harbor Gallery, Gig Harbor, Wash.

February 1998 — "Seeing Through" two-person show, Goldman Art Gallery, Rockville, Md.

December 1997 — Glass Ornament Collection for White House Christmas tree, Washington, D.C.

June 1996 — Olympic Games Goblet Invitational, Vesperman Gallery, Atlanta, Ga.

May 1995 — "In Women We Trust," Vitrum Gallery, Asheville, N.C.

April 1994 — "Art of Helping Award," presented to Boeing Company, American Red Cross, Seattle, Wash.

May 1994 — Featured artist, Ikebana International, Seattle University, Seattle, Wash.

May 1994 — "All That Glitters," Mockingbird Gallery, Bend, Ore.

June 1993 — "A Touch of Flameworked Glass and More," Ariana Gallery, Birmingham, Mont.

1993 — Northwest Women in Glass, Kirsten Gallery, Seattle, Wash.

1992 — Goblets 1992, Mindscape Gallery, Evanston, Il.

1992 — International Exhibition of Glass, Kanazawa, Ishikawa, Japan.

1992 — Corning Museum of Glass, New Glass Review 13, Corning, N.Y.

November 1992 — "Off The Wall," American Craft Council Juried Auction, New York City, N.Y.

1990 — International Exhibition of Glass, Ishikawa, Japan.

I call my father, the neurosurgeon. "Dad, I think Jay is alive. Maybe in his shame from falling off the wagon, he hitchhiked out of town and ran away. Maybe he's living on the streets of L.A. with thousands of homeless people, drinking and doing drugs. He needs our help."

"Narda, Jay died from his head injury," my father says. "My guess is that his brain bled, and he died in the afternoon. Instead of doing the right thing and calling the police, Kurt and Cat hid Jay's body."

"But they passed the lie detector test, Dad!"

He must be wrong. We would have found Jay's body by now.

Determined to resist my father's confidence that Jay is dead, I suddenly have new, hopeful resolve that he is alive.

All winter I continue to search for Jay, but now I look outside of our town. I scan faces on TV—people watching parades and at sporting events, or crowded outside the window of shows like *Good Morning America*. I go to San Francisco to visit my aunt Judith, and I search the airports, the streets, the restaurants.

I beg the universe to place me in Jay's path.

When the snow melts the following spring, a local man contacts the police. He tells them he heard someone in a bar saying that Jay died while hanging out with some bad people, and they hid his body in a mineshaft.

What if this man heard correctly?

Two of my friends, Jim and Jack, help me search the mines, mostly out the East Fork of the Big Wood River. One mine is vertical. Jim drops a rock and waits for the sound of the splash at the bottom. *One-one thousand, two-one thousand, three-one thousand, four-one thousand ...* splash. The three of us stare at each other in shock. Could Jay be at the bottom?

Search and Rescue contacts the Mountain Home air force base and hires a technician with a special extension camera to search the mine. The camera is removed from the foam protection in its hard case. A thick, black plastic cord is securely attached to the camera. As the camera is lowered into the mine, the cord is carefully unwound from a large metal spool. On a small screen, we view the sides of the cave.

I watch the screen with a mix of anticipation and dread. Suddenly, I can't breathe. It's silent as all eyes stay glued to the monitor. The minutes tick away slowly and then, abruptly, the cord stops. The technician sighs and says, "We've hit the water. I'm sorry, this mine is clear." Another failed search.

That night I dream we're searching in a forest where the trees are far apart and the ground is soft with leaves. Up ahead, people stand around looking into a cave. As I approach, they look at me, shake their heads and then divert their eyes. I see two legs sticking out of the mouth of the cave opening and I stop. My heart sinks. Suddenly, Jay is standing next to me. He hugs me and says, "I'm so sorry, Narda. I'm so sorry."

I'm awakened by the pressure of Jay's arms around me.

We've been searching for nine months. When we don't find Jay's body, I decide he's alive. *God, I miss him. The way we've been searching clearly isn't working. If he's alive, why hasn't he come home? And how will I ever find him?*

I can't continue to track down every lead, search every nook and cranny, every stream and forest in Idaho—much less across the country, across the world. I'm just one person. Even with a search team behind me, there's only so much ground we can cover. I know the world is too big. Too vast. I feel frustrated, powerless.

Then a crazy thought hits me. Just like the press conferences people hold that call attention to their missing loved ones, could I put my voice out there, too? But what if—instead—I could take it a step further? What if I do something so incredible, so amazing, that it would lure

Jay back home? I'm certain he's alive. Perhaps he just felt ashamed. As someone in the public arena, I could use that platform to put myself in the spotlight. And, in turn, somehow find a way to bring him back.

When I share these thoughts with other people, I can tell they sense that I'm a little crazy. But I feel desperate about Jay's disappearance, the giant hole he's left in my life and my helplessness, because I can't figure out the puzzle.

I think of my strengths and talents—what could propel me forward? I'm good at real estate, but that's not an industry that will bring fame. I've traveled extensively, so perhaps I could write a book about my adventures.

Nothing is stirring me, nothing feels inspiring. But then, I remember Japanese. I learned to read the characters so quickly—why? Several in my family, including Jay, had struggled with reading. And so many across the U.S. struggle, too, leading to worrisome rates of crime and imprisonment among challenged readers. Could the system in Japan for teaching Japanese be adapted to English? And might that be my ticket to fame?

Jay will hear about me on a radio show, or see me on TV. He will want to come home. And, if I develop a system that really works, maybe he could finally learn to read the way he's always wanted to.

I'm consumed with guilt over what I could have done. If only I had taken him by the hand that last night and gone directly to a recovery meeting instead of believing he'd make his drinks weak. Maybe now, finding a way to do something really helpful for people could lead me back to him.

Chapter 19

Hiragana for English

I'm headed to the elementary school a couple of blocks from my home to speak to Ilene, the reading specialist who helped Sadie learn to read two years ago. Ilene has time to teach me the sounds of English, and I learn that, even though we have only 26 letters in our alphabet, our language has 38 sounds!

Back at the house, Sadie joins me at the dining room table. I take out a stack of three-by-five index cards and have Sadie count out 38 of them. Together, Sadie and I write each of the 38 sounds Ilene taught me in the upper-left corner of a card. Then, we figure out which cards get which of the 26 letters of the English alphabet. To my amazement, I realize that 12 of our 26 letters have just one sound, while the other 14 have multiple sounds.

Sadie is confused by the multiple sounds 14 letters make.

I tell her, "You know, Sadie, when I lived in Japan in my 20s, I learned to read Japanese in a week."

"Come on, Mama, that's ridiculous."

"Really," I tell her. "There's an ingenious way to learn to read in Japanese called *Hiragana*. Simple symbols appear underneath the two thousand complicated *Kanji*, so everyone knows what sound to make. Japanese is so much easier to learn than English, even though English has far fewer letters."

"We need *Hiragana* for English, Mama."

I smile. "That's right, Sadie. And that's what we're creating."

I know if I adapt *Hiragana* to English, many illiterate people will, for the first time in their lives, easily learn to read. How fantastic! I'll be interviewed on TV and, surely, Jay will see me. I'll help many people, and my reward will be Jay—on my couch, home safe and sound.

Jay's grin from ear to ear is the image I fix in my mind.

In the days that follow, I pull out the 38 cards that Sadie and I have made. Analyzing them, I realize I'll need 12 symbols in total. In order to keep my system to only 12 symbols, I'll need to use a letter to represent a sound, when possible. So, I put a "z" under the "s" in "is," "was," and "always."

$$\underset{z}{\text{i}\underset{z}{\text{s}}} \quad \text{wa}\underset{z}{\text{s}} \quad \text{alway}\underset{z}{\text{s}}$$

In this way, I have clearly identified the sounds that *need* symbols. I create 12 symbols using simple shapes: square, triangle, diamond, dots, lines and so on. The square symbol lives under the "ch" in "chair," "chess" and "cheese." It also lives under the "t" in "future" and "nature." Students will see the square symbol under the "ch" or the "t" and know what sound to make.

$$\underset{\square}{\text{ch}}\text{air} \quad \underset{\square}{\text{ch}}\text{ess} \quad \underset{\square}{\text{ch}}\text{eese} \quad \text{fu}\underset{\square}{\text{t}}\text{ure} \quad \text{na}\underset{\square}{\text{t}}\text{ure}$$

I call on my friend Helen to look over my work and make suggestions. Helen and I met many years ago when she and her husband moved to our area and needed a real estate agent. She has short, sandy-brown hair and hazel eyes—windows to her deeply spiritual soul. Her kindness draws me in, and I hike, ski or have lunch with her—anything just to be near her. She is easily the smartest person I know. She is a good listener and insightful. Helen enthusiastically agrees to help however she can. She reviews everything, confirming the 38 sounds of English and tweaking the 12 symbols.

I take a mock-up of my creation to Barge Levy, a Sun Valley local well known in town for teaching reading in prisons.

After reviewing my idea, he says, "Drop everything you're doing and focus on this project. You will make a huge difference in the world. Now get going."

With great excitement, I call Mom and tell her my plan to lure Jay home. "I'll call it Narda … Narda-something, so if Jay isn't watching, he'll hear 'Narda,' and it'll catch his attention."

Mom is up for a new plan to find Jay. We all are tormented by not knowing where he is.

"How about *Nardagani?*" Mom says. "It kind of rhymes with *origami* and sounds like a combination of *Hiragana* and *Kanji* of your name."

Maybe this is why I've endured such an odd name all my life—we need it now.

At last, I have a focus for my attention. The void that is my despair and confusion—my depression—is partially filled.

Soon after Jay's disappearance, I start smoking marijuana and drinking more than usual. I'm looking for numbness, escape from the confusion of my lost brother, and the fear that he could be in a bad place with mean people. The nightmare goes on in my mind all day, relentlessly. Marijuana takes the edge off my pain.

I start drinking while making dinner for the kids during the weeks they're with me. Then the weeks they're not with me. Sometimes I have a tequila and orange juice with lunch to get me through the afternoon.

A friend offers me some medicinal marijuana to lift my spirits, claiming it's for depression. It works; I feel lighter. So, I begin jump-starting my day with a puff. Some days, when I feel the depression grabbing hold too tightly, I puff all day, every couple of hours. The correlation of Mom's and Jay's drug and alcohol abuse, and now mine, doesn't enter my mind. I'm simply running from the pain any way I can.

Now, all I want to do is work on Nardagani. Completely lost in time, I work tirelessly. Many of my friends and family don't understand this outside-the-box system I'm creating. After all, I'm not an educator. They think I've lost my mind.

"Narda, wake up," they say. "Stop this craziness. You have children. Go back to real estate or get a job. Come back to reality."

I hear this from countless people. But I don't get a job. I hole up at home. *My plan will work.*

With tremendous faith in my financial future, because this program is going to help millions of people, I live frugally and lean on my home equity line of credit and credit cards. In this way, my focus stays fully on Nardagani. The worst-case scenario is that I may have to sell my house.

I call the local TV station and ask if they'll interview me. I'm excited to talk publicly about the Nardagani Reading Program I've created—somehow, Jay might hear me. I tell myself that any contact with Jay would be useful. If he's hiding out in shame, he might have to hear me or see me several times before he's reminded of my love, and the safety of home.

Meanwhile, I've developed a Sound Map—a list of the 38 sounds in English. The Sound Map clearly indicates all of the sounds, especially the 14 letters that "don't play fair" and have multiple sounds. I've also developed a game to help memorize the symbols, and a short story coded with the symbols, so students can practice reading and build their confidence. The TV station agrees to interview me. It goes well; I feel confident and articulate.

The day after my interview airs, a local business owner and acquaintance approaches me and whispers in my ear, "I saw you on TV. I can't read."

My knees buckle. This is my first connection to a struggling reader outside of my family. I keep my composure and say, "Give me your number. I'll call you tomorrow. I'll teach you my program."

"Promise me you won't say anything to anyone?" he asks.

I give him my word.

I teach him to read in two weeks. And, to my surprise and delight, once he's confident reading with the symbols and sounding out words, he no longer needs the symbols. In Japanese, the *Hiragana* symbols appear under the *Kanji* nearly everywhere. But in English, the symbols are just like training wheels on a bike, eventually removed for uninhibited forward motion.

I teach a second person, then a third. I can see them coming. They look left and right to make sure nobody is watching as they approach me and whisper, "I can't read." Each student offers a new perspective on teaching the program, and I adjust. I change the order of the Sound Map, add a homework sheet, a Memory Match game and Bingo. In less than three months, I teach seven adults in our community to read. These are people I never suspected of being "unable to read."

In a dream, I'm invited to be on *The Oprah Winfrey Show*. Oprah and I are sitting on her couch in the middle of the stage. She's asking me questions about Jay and the Nardagani Reading Program. She tells me, "I have a surprise for you," and Jay walks out from behind the curtain. Bursting into tears and hugging him with all my strength, I say, "It's over, it's over ... I've found you, Jay!"

I wake up with a feeling of hope.

Chapter 20

Help with Nardagani

It's been three years since Jay disappeared. I'm still obsessed with finding him through Nardagani. My next plan is to create a book to code with the Nardagani symbols, a book long enough so students have a chance to sit and read for a long while. I come up with the idea to write about things people have in common—relationships, money, food, exercise, sleep, and thoughts.

"Okay, Universe, please help me."

And the Universe seems to respond. My pencil begins to move and write and charge forward. I'm flooded with thoughts and ideas. Inspirations occur all day and all evening. Thoughts float into my mind that won't leave me alone until they are down on paper. This must be God, or some power making this happen, because it's not me. I'm the follower, simply taking the notes as fast as I can.

Soon I have paper and pencil in every room of the house—next to my bed, the kitchen counter, next to the toilet, in my purse, in my car. I try to write while hiking and rollerblading, but this becomes a nuisance. I buy a tape recorder and dictate while on foot or rolling down the path.

It takes all my concentration to compile and type up so many small pieces of paper and to transcribe the voice recordings into chapters on my computer. Printing several pages at a time, I go over them carefully. One day my son Raleigh, almost 11, picks the writing up off my desk.

"If you're teaching people to read, why do you make it complicated by saying, the *theme* of this chapter is food? Why not just say, 'This chapter is about food'?"

"You're right, that's much easier. Will you sit with me and look at the first couple of pages?"

On the first page, Raleigh finds four places to simplify my writing. On the second page, he finds five. He makes a deal with me for a dollar per page and gets to work with a red pen. After I have incorporated Raleigh's updates, Helen does a final edit.

Around the same time, I meet a local man touted as a computer genius, Todd Mandeville. Todd uses a software program to create the Nardagani font, which places my special symbols under the letters that "don't play fair."

"Two years ago there wasn't a program that could make this specialized font. Lucky timing," he says.

Todd also builds a database to store all the words we code with our symbols. He's been on a team of translators and coders. He wrote software programs that translated programs in other languages, like Japanese and Chinese. Todd tells me, "I never would have guessed I'd be using this specialized type of program again. This is amazing, really."

He estimates that, for the scope of this project, it may cost as much as $20,000 to develop the whole thing. *What? How will I come up with that?*

After I have cashed in my retirement account, Todd begins to build the program with me by his side.

I tell him, "We're building a way to show the 12 symbols under the letters that do not play fair, so that struggling readers will know the correct sound to make when they see the symbols.

We need to be able to put two lines *and* three lines under 'th,' because 'th' makes two different sounds. Try it. Say 'three' out loud. Okay, now say 'then' out loud—feel the difference? I tell my students that the third line is for extra vibration."

three   then

"Now we need to put two dots under the 'o' and also two dots under the 'a' because the *same sound* is made by both the 'o' and the 'a.'"

o̤ften ca̤ll

Sadie, now 11 years old, says she'll draw pictures to go with the stories. "Okay," I say. "Draw a couple and let's see how you do."

They are adorable. Sadie draws her little heart out and our book comes alive with color.

Chapter 21

A Slippery Slope

Following Jay's disappearance in 2001, Mom holds on the best she can for the next four years. But really, the family has splintered and shattered in confusion and sadness. Without closure, without really knowing what's happened, we're constantly waiting, always in purgatory.

Mom calls me on New Year's Day, 2005. It seems she and Walt have stopped going to recovery meetings. "Walter and I did a bad thing last night. We went to the Space Needle and drank a glass of champagne."

"Oh Mom, that was dumb. Get to a recovery meeting today."

Normally, Mom would call me a couple of times a week. But then she stops calling me and rarely answers her phone. In late January, I decide to load up the kids and drive to Kirkland to visit her. We arrive in the afternoon. Sadie and Raleigh want to play with Walter, who has built a track in the backyard for remote control cars. Mom and I drive to pick up AJ, who has moved with Jenny to Mount Vernon, about an hour north of Seattle.

When we arrive back at Mom's, Sadie and Raleigh run out to the car to greet us. Sadie cries, "Mom, Walter is being mean. He told us to go away. He went to his room and slammed the door."

"Okay … Well, why don't you three play in the backyard while Sue-Sue and I make dinner?" Mom had decided to be called Grandma Sue.

But when Sadie was just old enough to begin talking, she began calling her Sue-Sue and the name stuck.

Walter doesn't join us for dinner. Later that evening, the kids and I settle into my room downstairs. We play a game of Apples to Apples and then we read until bedtime. We head off to sleep.

The next morning, all three kids are shaking me. "Mom, wake up! There's been an earthquake! Come upstairs and see."

My heart jolts. It's pounding in my chest as we go up the stairs. Standing at the top, everywhere I look, Mom's lovely glass art pieces are shattered and broken. Mom is in the living room, sobbing, her head in her hands.

"I'm not sure how much more I can take of Walter's drinking. I've tried to get us back to meetings, but he refuses. Walter says terribly mean things to me. He swears like you wouldn't believe."

Suddenly, we hear Walter coughing. He's coming down the hall from the bedroom. He stands at the edge of the living room. His eyes widen and his jaw drops in disbelief. He lunges for the front door, slamming it on his way out. We do not see him again.

We stay a few days, but everything is awkward, and I can tell Mom is uncomfortable. She's sad. I'm on high alert, wondering if she's drinking. She doesn't seem to be.

Mom wants to clear out closets and cupboards, take everything possible to the Goodwill. I help her. Richard comes by and stays to do everything he can to entertain the kids, bring us food and lighten Mom's mood.

Finally, it's time to head back to Idaho. I'm anxious about leaving Mom, but convince myself all will be well, especially with Richard living close by.

Weeks go by, and Mom doesn't answer her phone when I call. She checks in occasionally to say that Walter is a bit better. She's convinced they'll make it through this rough patch. Given everything, I'm not so sure.

I'm going through my own rough patch, with a man I've been dating for nearly four years. As with all my relationships, when Vance began to show interest in me, I became interested in him. He approached me at Ketch'em Alive, a free music event in Ketchum that happens every Tuesday evening all summer long. He is kind. We dance until the music ends.

Vance is short and stocky, with curly blonde hair and engaging green eyes. He's a construction worker who moved to Ketchum from Las Vegas for a job three years earlier, and never left.

Being an environmentalist, Vance advocates for the protection of the earth. He teaches me the finer points of recycling—where our recycling goes, how it gets processed, and how it's made into products.

Vermicomposting is another of his passions; composting with a special kind of worm that wants to be domesticated and eat our food scraps. The worm's poop, called castings, is the richest fertilizer in the world. In his garage is a worm bin made simply from a large cardboard box lined with thick plastic. Moistened newspapers are the bedding for the worms, and food scraps, which would otherwise go into the garbage, is their food. Farmers who use castings from these worms are finding their yields are up by a third, and the need for water is down by a third, because the castings enrich the soil and bring it back to life so that it can retain water more efficiently. I'm enthralled with these progressive ways to care for Mother Earth.

Vance and I mountain bike and hike in the summer; we enjoy each other's company through the fall. When winter arrives, we snowboard and snowshoe.

I get triggered and angry, but we work through it. Vance tells me he wants to help me understand why I am this way. We patiently talk through the drama.

Two years into our relationship, Vance wants to move in with me. I say it would be odd for me to live with my boyfriend—I don't want to set the wrong example for my young children. Next thing I know, he pops the question, and is holding out a stunning engagement ring. I love Vance, and I'm ready to have a man in my life at this point. I think about it overnight. *Maybe my love will grow stronger after being engaged.* Vance likes to drink, so that works, because I do, too, but I will have to hide my smoking because he thinks I do it too much.

I decide to say yes. *I guess it's okay to live with my fiancé?*

It's late February. I've just gotten the kids off to school. I'm making my bed when the phone rings. I hear panic in Mom's voice.

"Please come help me, Narda. I'm scared. Walt is saying the most horrible things, he's scaring me. I need to do something. I need help."

"I'll throw some things in a suitcase and head your way within the hour."

I go downstairs. Vance is at the kitchen table with his coffee and the newspaper.

"I'm heading to Seattle. Mom's in trouble. Will you watch the kids until they go to their dad's house in a couple of days?"

"Are you kidding me? This is ridiculous," says Vance. "Call her back. She can't be so dependent on you. She's a grown woman!"

He continues, "This is an example of what I've been trying to tell you, about codependence!"

I snap back at him. "Codependence is an excessive reliance on another person. She's always been independent! She's never asked me for help!"

Flustered, confused, and ultimately swayed by his comments, I call Mom back. "I can't come today. I'll get the kids to Eric's on Friday and drive out the next morning."

On Friday, my brother Richard calls. "Have you heard from Mom?"

"I talked with her a couple of days ago, why?"

"She and I were supposed to blow glass yesterday, but she wasn't around. I stopped by again this morning, but there's no sign of Mom or Walter. Walter's van is gone."

I try to stay calm. My last conversation with Mom is fresh in my mind.

The next day, still no word from her. We know something is terribly wrong. Do we call the police about our missing 67-year-old mother?

I feel the familiar panic and fear. Do I get in my car and drive to Seattle to search for her?

That night, Mom comes to me in a vivid dream. She wants to show me something. We travel across the Universe, through the brightness of the Milky Way, to the far side of existence. Mom explains, "When we die, we have choices. You can incarnate to one of these four planets. All are peaceful places where we live in harmony. There are no wars and there's plenty of food for everyone. If you want to be an animal, you can incarnate to that far planet," she says, pointing to the smallest one.

Mom takes my hand, pulls me back through the brilliant mass of stars and across the ether. We hover on a cloud, looking down at the lights twinkling on our world. "Earth is the hardest place to live. People choose it to learn lessons, to be teachers, and to help others. Another choice is to stay in angel form. I'll be guiding you. Watch for me."

I startle awake with a surreal sense of foreboding and dread. I lie there for hours, staring at the ceiling and thinking about my mother. *Where are you, Mom?*

The next morning, still dazed, I manage to click into autopilot to get the kids off to school, then get myself showered and dressed. I'm thankful for an 11 a.m. appointment with my therapist.

As I'm about to walk in, my cell phone rings. It's Richard. His voice is low and trembling, "Mom's gone."

"What do you mean, *gone?*"

"She died three days ago. Walter called me this morning from the county jail."

My whole body floods with adrenalin. Panicked, I run down the hall to the bathroom. My head is spinning as I vomit into the toilet. I'm gagging and sobbing uncontrollably. Realizing I still have the phone in my hand, I choke out a few words, "Need to get home ... call you back."

Grabbing a large handful of toilet paper, I hold it over my face, walk into my therapist's office and say, "Mom died. I'm going home."

Driving and bawling in a frenzy, somehow I make the 10 short blocks and park the car in my garage.

Oh, my God! What have I done? What did I do by not going to help my mother when she asked me for help?

Desperate to know more, I call Richard back. He tells me what Walter told him, that they went to a musical in downtown Seattle. On the way home they stopped at a bar for a nightcap. The next thing Walter remembers is waking up in jail. It was morning. The guard wouldn't give Walter any information or let him call his wife. Later that day, a court-ordered attorney visited him and told him Susan was in the morgue at the hospital. The lawyer said Walter could use the phone, but he was too confused and mortified to call anyone.

I take to my bed, hoping for sleep and a respite from this horror. Paralyzed with self-loathing, I lie there, believing my life will be filled with despair until my death. I want to call Mom, hear her voice. *Please God, let me turn back the clock.*

Hours later, the kids come home from school. I hear Sadie's voice, "Mom, we're home!"

Dread engulfs me. How will I tell my two middle-school-aged children that I have killed their grandma? Footsteps run up the stairs. The door swings wide and two sets of puzzled eyes lock on mine. They walk over slowly and sit on the bed. Through my tears, I tell them that Grandma Sue-Sue has died. Sadie begins to cry, too. Raleigh stares at me with shock on his face and asks, "How?"

"We don't really know yet. She and Walter were out at night and there was an accident."

"A car accident?"

All I can do is cry and say, "I don't know."

Later that afternoon I call Vance at work. I tell him the news, and the next thing I know I'm yelling out of control through the phone. He says he'll stay with his buddy for the night and hangs up on me.

Eric comes over with take-out. "Look kids, you're coming with me for a while. Mom's going to Seattle to be with her brothers."

The next morning, I drive the 11 hours to Seattle. My self-loathing is like a snake, slowly tightening its grip. *If I had made this drive one week ago, Mom would still be alive.*

According to the police report, when Mom and Walter stopped for a nightcap, they both got drunk. Walter was belligerent when the bartender refused to serve him another drink. On the way out of the bar, Mom fell down three steps. She lay there unconscious while Walter shouted at her to get up. When she came to, Walter ushered her into their white Dodge van.

The bartender watched as Walter helped Mom into the passenger seat, then he saw him walk across the parking lot into another bar. Fearing Mom was hurt, the bartender called 911. When the ambulance arrived, she was unconscious. The paramedics performed CPR as they raced her to the emergency room, but they couldn't revive her.

The autopsy says she died of "positional asphyxia." Her airway was blocked by how she was positioned in the van.

I'm heartbroken. When I was young, I didn't know my mother and all that she did for us children. Now I'm older, and she and I become friends for the first time in my life. Then she dies.

The next week, Sadie and Raleigh fly to Seattle for the memorial service. We hold it at the Kirkland Arts Center, the site of Mom's wedding five years earlier. Her many friends make all the preparations. The Ikebana ladies create magnificent flower arrangements to make the setting beautiful. All the chairs are filled, and people crowd around the perimeter. It's a long service. Many want to speak.

Mom's sister, Judith, has everyone in tears of laughter when she shares stories of their sweet relationship. "When I was younger and living in San Francisco, a long-term relationship ended. I moved into an apartment by myself. I was devastated. Susan sent me a different housewarming card every day for a month to cheer me up."

Then, just as quickly, Judith has everyone in tears of sorrow as the grief of losing such a remarkable confidante sets in. As Judith sits down after speaking, I see she is shaking her head, tears streaming down her cheeks. Her flowing blonde hair shines in the sunlight coming through the window. At that moment, I so appreciate her courage. Judith is dear to me; we've always had a special relationship. I see her as a role model, a woman to emulate. Her strength is also my strength; I can feel it flowing through her despite our overwhelming sadness. Hearing her kind words and being in her presence is a comfort.

A small group of Japanese women surrounds the eldest Ikebana leader as she reads in Japanese from a letter she has written. A younger woman translates. She reads about how much they loved Mom's gentle spirit. Mom was the only foreigner in their group, yet she fit right in with her enthusiasm for the art of flower arranging and her ever-improving Japanese language skills.

There are whispers around the room as a gentleman I don't recognize steps to the front. "I've been an auctioneer for fundraisers in the Northwest for 26 years. I've never experienced a person more giving than Susan. We've lost an amazingly creative, generous woman."

Sadie, 12 years old, stands up and turns around to face the crowd. "Grandma Sue-Sue was the kindest person. Last summer we were at the Seattle Center in the food court. There was a homeless man sitting at a table nearby. Sue-Sue offered to buy him lunch and she asked him what he wanted most. When she returned with his tray of food, it was piled really high."

As for Mom's affairs, she had revised her will a month earlier. It stipulates that we are to sell her house and stocks, and the money is to be divided six ways between Dave, Tom, Richard, and me, Jay's son AJ, and Walter.

Although Walter's involvement in the circumstances surrounding Mom's death is difficult to think about, I know that Mom loved him deeply. And that brings me peace. She felt real love for the first time in her life because of Walter. I feel sure that if she hadn't loved him so much, she wouldn't have revised her will that way. Mom and Walter fell off the wagon together. She wouldn't want him to suffer in prison while she watches from heaven.

Nobody has seen or heard from Walter since Mom's death.

Back home in Idaho, my guilt and grief are agonizing. In this horrendous condition, I hang onto my ever-eroding relationship with Vance. I fear another loss may kill me.

It's spring in Ketchum and people are walking with a skip in their step. There are happy people everywhere, oblivious to the tragedy in my life. How is it that the world can just go on, like nothing has happened?

Four months after Mom's death, for Vance's 40th birthday, I surprise him with his dream car—a brand new Honda Element in his favorite color, green. I buy it with my recent inheritance from Mom. Five months later, we break up. Vance takes his Element and moves out of my home.

Despite everything, I'm having a hard time coming to terms with the end of this relationship. I miss looking into his brilliant green eyes and feeling the comfort of his body next to mine in the night. I hang on to the fantasy that we might get back together after some time apart. Maybe he'll realize how great I am because I gave him the car of his dreams for his birthday, and come back to me. I don't really want him back; I'm just so lost and lonely. The car morphs into something it never was before—a symbol of our relationship, a talisman of what could have been, our last link. At the same time, it's also a financial asset that I need. I think about asking him to return the Element, or at least pay me for it, but I'm afraid this may shut the door on the relationship forever.

I'm devastated. For the next two years, I rarely leave my house. My smoking and drinking reach an all-time high. What focus I have is on further developing Nardagani. As I go to bed each night, I pray, "Mom, please help me find Jay." With two of those I hold dearest gone, part of me wonders who could be next.

Chapter 22

On the Run

It's 2006, and our family is imploding. My sweet daughter Sadie, once at the top of her class, is now lost and struggling. How can I blame her? Her closest uncle is missing, her grandmother extraordinaire has died tragically, and now her mother is crippled by depression.

Speeding headlong into her teens, Sadie turns to drugs and alcohol, too. It's a family inheritance I wish I could put an end to. All I can think of is Jay and Mom, now gone because of the disease of alcoholism. I'm afraid for Sadie's future. Will she be able to escape the cycle?

Midway through eighth grade, Sadie gets caught supplying a popular over-the-counter drug to her middle-school friend. Both she and the friend are expelled for the rest of the school year. Sadie reminds me of Jay at this age. The tightness in my chest will not release. My jaw is sore from clenching my teeth in anxiety. I don't want this for her.

"School is a waste of time, Mama. It's boring."

Within the first month of being expelled from school, Sadie has three paying jobs—assisting a baker in the early morning, working at a deli for lunch, and cleaning houses with our dear friend, Jen Rush. I've known Jen for many years. She's petite with long black hair, bangs and faint freckles on her light skin. Jen has an optimistic spirit and surprises me often with her nuggets of wisdom.

Biking is Sadie's mode of travel in every kind of weather. "This life is much more satisfying than school," she often tells me.

Throughout spring and summer, Sadie is at peace with being expelled. She seems to be back on track.

In July, Sadie asks Eric and me if she can attend a course with NOLS, National Outdoor Leadership School. Eric and I agree this is a good idea. For the last month of summer, Sadie joins a group of 15 teenagers in the Wind River Range, in Wyoming. For 30 days they're mostly above treeline, traversing the wilderness off-trail, rock climbing, learning wilderness medicine and developing leadership skills. Ice-climbing equipment is hauled up each time they attempt a summit. Food is packed in on horses and mules when it's time to resupply.

The facilitator tells me later that even though Sadie was the youngest of the group, at 13, she took on a leadership role.

I love that she's growing, and I'm hungry for more ways we can fuel her strengths. Has it been inside her all along? Or something we did as parents? And if it was inside all along, why did she get expelled from eighth grade? Why didn't she lead there?

Several parents with kids a bit older than Sadie had told me that our public schools are terrific because the teachers are young and excited to educate their students. But some of the teachers are old and tired, just getting through to retirement. They expressed worry about this dynamic.

Could the weary teachers have had something do to with Sadie being bored and restless in school, leading to trouble?

In the fall, when ninth grade begins, so do the problems with drugs and alcohol.

Eric calls me to discuss the situation. "I can't watch her do this anymore. I've done some research and I'm taking her to a lockdown treatment center for kids her age. We leave in three days."

God, at this point I'm willing to try anything.

Bachelor Academy is a residential treatment center in the mountains near Bend, Oregon. Sadie hates it. When we see her again, many months later, she tells us of her horrific experiences, like being kept awake for 30 hours with a group of 20 or more kids in a hut. Hunger stabbed at her gut and created tremendous fear.

The counselor in charge had told them to get into a character that portrayed their deepest shame and to act as this person for everyone to see. This was just one of many techniques to "break" these kids, Sadie tells us later. We have no idea this is happening. "We'll call you with updates," they said, but those calls never came.

Two months after Eric delivers Sadie to Bachelor Academy, I get a call from them early in the morning. "Sadie's run away. We highly recommend you call the local bounty hunter."

"What? How can this be?"

"It happens. Here's the phone number to call. Good luck."

After I call, we wait. Raleigh and I are at home, pacing. We're terrified by what the bounty hunter tells us—that if he doesn't catch Sadie, she could be on the run for a long time. I'm frightened.

Eric checks in every hour. "Any word? Sorry, I know you'd call if there were any news. I'll be over after work with a pizza."

I imagine the bounty hunter driving up and down the cold mountain road. "The sub-zero temperatures will flush her out of the woods," he told me on the phone earlier in the day. "Cold holds tightly in the trees. With the frigid temperatures, she'll get very tired. The treatment center is 25 miles into the national forest—it's nearly impossible to escape. We usually catch them by midnight."

My Sadie. She's only 13!

An old, familiar feeling of anxiety and fear courses through my body. I'm reminded of Nikki and Ratto, Jay and Mom. Now the searching is to find my daughter. My heart is pounding and the skin all over my body is tight. *Not again!*

At midnight, Raleigh and I head to our bedrooms, exhausted.

The sound of my phone ringing is loud in the wee hours of the morning. The bounty hunter is on the line. "We've got her. She's shaken, but okay. We'll transport her to Prineville now. Tomorrow, you'll need to decide what to do with her."

On the drive to Prineville, Sadie says to the bounty hunter, "It's a horrible place. I won't go back."

Eric and I are completely appalled at the situation. We pull ourselves together to do some quick research. I make calls. He researches online. We want to find a better place for Sadie.

Three months after Sadie's escape, Bachelor Academy is shut down for abusive practices.

Eric and I find a therapeutic wilderness program based in Duchesne, Utah, called Second Nature. It's touted as the most challenging and effective wilderness program in America, especially during the winter months. Sadie is transported to their headquarters the next day. It's right before Thanksgiving.

"Send your daughter nothing for the holidays. Nothing!" they tell us. We can visit in a month or so.

Finally, in late January, I get a call. A woman from Second Nature tells me that only one parent at a time can come to visit. Two days later, I head out early in the morning for the five-hour drive to Duchesne. Arriving at the headquarters, I board a Hummer-type vehicle with two other moms. The mood is somber as the vehicle jostles us around for two and a half hours through the snow. We go deep into the wilderness. The constant, erratic jolting makes me carsick.

Suddenly, we burst out from the thick forest above the treeline, into wide open space with snow as far as I can see.

It's late morning when we pull up next to a makeshift camp. There's a large tarp over a fire, and a crude kitchen is set up on the far side. Scattered around the area are smaller tarps tied to the few trees sticking up from the ground—the sleeping quarters.

The six girls at camp don't know we are coming. It's a surprise for them to see us. And it's a shock for us to see the grime on their faces and hands, even though they've washed up for a surprise. We all sit under the shelter on logs and blankets around the fire. The taste of hot tea is soothing.

Awkwardness hangs in the air as we introduce ourselves. The girls seem weary and sad, with dust on their necks, their hair knotted and greasy. Once in pretty clothes, now they have chapped lips and thick dirt under their fingernails.

It's strange to be here, a place I could never have imagined in my wildest dreams. My daughter sits on the other side of the fire with the girls, while I sit with the moms. My eyes move to Sadie, beautiful under all the grime, vibrant. Is the leader in Sadie I learned about last summer still in there? Is she searching for her place in the world?

The lead facilitator asks us to stretch our legs and come back for lunch "when we call you." Sadie and I walk to the edge of the camp, just far enough so we can talk without being heard.

"Mama," she says, "this is a good place for me. Yesterday we came back to this camp from a three-day solo—the first time they haven't taken my boots away at night."

My tears freeze onto my face in the minus-seven-degree temperature. I'm grateful to be with Sadie and yet mortified by our situation. I wonder how we got here.

Sadie tells me about being up on the top of the world, solo. They brought her—blindfolded—to a designated area where she had to stay. It was within sight of the main tent. Because of the deep snow, they would be able to tell if she left. She wrote, read, and did stretches to stay warm under her tarp. Every night and morning they checked on her and brought her food and water for the day.

Sadie hands me a book, *Man's Search for Meaning* by Viktor Frankl. "I read this during my solo. He was in a German concentration camp. He wrote about the physical hardships. The conditions were terrible, but nobody could touch his mind. He had to change his thinking to survive.

"Like us, Mama, with our recent family tragedies. We need to rehabilitate our thinking. Things aren't the same. My life is forever changed, Mama. I don't want to do drugs and drink alcohol to escape anymore. I want to help people who are going through distress like me. This program is amazing. Thank you for sending me here."

Sadie has become conscious of her actions and their consequences. She wants to be a better person and figure things out. She can see her mistakes for what they are and she wants to change.

I sigh and finger the lip balm in my pocket. What a surprise to know that Sadie is happy in this desolate place, in the high desert of Utah.

She continues. "Some parts of being here are really hard. We break down camp and walk every day for hours through thigh-deep snow. We're never told when we'll stop or when we'll eat. We carry everything on our backs, even the tarp we sleep under. When the sun is low in the sky, we stop to set up a new camp for the night. A couple of the girls cry all the time."

"You're so strong," I manage to say, as my heart sinks and I reach for the support of a lone tree next to me.

"Get this, Mama—when I go to the bathroom, I have to yell my name over and over so they can keep track of me. It's humiliating, but shouting 'Sadie, Sadie, Sadie' feels good in my throat."

We laugh and my heart lightens. Even though she's only 13, I catch a glimpse of the fierce and wonderful woman she could become.

Pulling the lip balm out of my pocket, I cautiously hand it over. The rule is that I am not allowed to bring *anything* to my daughter. Sadie looks around, and quickly soothes her dry lips.

"The whole program is based around the four elements: earth, fire, water, and air. The first is earth. When I arrived, the goal was for me to get grounded. I wasn't allowed to talk at all. I hiked behind the rest of the group. I sat at my own fire while the group sat around a group fire. They instructed me to write my life's story. When it was finished, I read my story to the group.

"Then fire. We have to make fire before we can eat warm food. I learned to use sagebrush and juniper to make a friction set that I can use to make fire. I worked so hard and ate so much cold food before I made my first fire."

I remember when Sadie learned to ride the unicycle in our driveway. It took her many hours of concentration to master. She was determined.

"Give me a tree, Mama, and I'll make you a fire! It's amazing how the instructors make us do that to build our self-confidence. So many kids, and people even, have never worked hard, failed and had to continue to work until they completed their goal.

"Now I'm working on the water element. I get to have more responsibility and use a knife. Air is the final step. After being out here, I think this life is simpler than the life you live back in town. I know I'll have to go back there, and even though there's running water and heat, I think living there is a bigger challenge than here. It's cold here, but it's such simple living, and so quiet. Hopefully, I can remember this place.

"Thank you for sending me here."

I pull a heart-shaped rock from my pocket and hand it to Sadie. "I found this on the edge of the river by our house. Merry Christmas. I can't get into trouble for bringing you a rock, right?"

We laugh, and my lungs open up for a deep, cold breath of air. Then Sadie tells me about PIES. It's a simple code word for a thorough check-in: "How are you? Physically, Intellectually, Emotionally, and Spiritually?"

I answer Sadie's question. "Physically, I feel strong. Snowboarding and snowshoeing keep me fit. Intellectually, I'm at an all-time high. With each person I teach to read, I discover a new way to improve Nardagani. It's incredibly stimulating work.

"Emotionally, I'm a wreck. What happened to my easy, simple life and my family? Depression drags me down. I never understood people with depression until Jay disappeared. Boy, do I get it now.

"Spiritually, well, I've been going to Light on the Mountains Center for Spiritual Living. It's an international faith community that has about 400 centers throughout the world. Reverend John Moreland taught me to meditate and he's teaching me how to be in the present moment, which creates much-needed calm in my life. When Jay disappeared, my world came tumbling down. Now I'm learning to see things with a fresh perspective—that I create my life with my thoughts and beliefs. But I'm developing this knowledge late in life, at 43 years old. It's phenomenal that you're acquiring clarity at 13!" I couldn't be prouder of my daughter.

Suddenly, we hear the others calling us. It's lunchtime.

Slowly, we crunch through the snow back to the group. Sitting in a tight circle around the warm fire, we eat a simple vegetable beef stew served up from a pot hanging above the hottest coals. Feelings of benevolence fill my soul as I sit in this sphere of individuals, all on a journey of valor.

I'm surprised when, after my last bite, the moms are asked to load up in the vehicle that brought us here. The field facilitator focuses his attention on the six girls and commands, "Ladies, pack up. We leave in 15 minutes."

No! Wait!

Sadie hugs me hard. I've just found her again. I don't want to leave.

Watching Sadie as our rig pulls away wrenches my heart. Riding along the rough road in silence, I think about our insightful conversation and what my own life could have been like with this remarkable opportunity to be in the wilderness. I wish every young person could have this chance at creative growth.

The road has been a difficult one for my young daughter, but in a way, I'm glad that those hard times led her to this place. She's learned something about herself, has had to push herself. Our conversation was one of mutual respect, of connection. I'm astounded by it—and so very grateful.

Two months later, when Sadie completes the wilderness program, an advisor at Second Nature suggests she attend Willow Creek School, a residential treatment program in Provo, Utah. We question this, but they insist it is the best strategy for her. Eric picks Sadie up from the headquarters in Duchesne and drives her there.

It's another lockdown facility, which means she can't leave unless escorted by a facilitator. If she does go out, she's strip-searched when she returns. *Oh my God, when will this phase of our lives be over?*

It's strange for Sadie to be locked indoors after being in the wilderness. Also, the facility used to be a nursing home, and so I think it must feel strangely like a hospital. *Is this environment really better for her?*

The academic classes at Willow Creek are not challenging for our now 14-year-old philosopher, but she loves the ice climbing, rock climbing, backpacking, and even a month-long trip to Vietnam. She's learning more about people and how she wants to live her life.

Willow Creek is a blessing, though I walk through my days in a haze of disbelief. People around me seem to be living normal lives, with kids at school locally. I wonder how I could have been—or could be—a better mother.

Nine months later, Willow Creek closes down—it has run out of funding.

Sadie has missed a whole year of high school, and we think it's not wise to bring her back home to continue. We do some research and find Lowell Whiteman, a boarding high school in the mountains near Steamboat, Colorado. The administrators review Sadie's application and her letters of recommendation. They're impressed by her leadership in the wilderness and agree to a Skype interview. Sadie is not officially accepted, but Eric picks her up from Willow Creek and drives her to Lowell Whiteman, hoping she'll get in. It's October, a month and a half after school has started. They say it will be very hard for her to catch up.

Chapter 23

Global Studies

Lowell Whiteman School accepts Sadie. She thrives in her newfound freedom, using the self-confidence she's gained to be thoroughly responsible. Within her first semester, and each semester after, Sadie earns an A in every subject. Lowell Whiteman has turned out to be a great transition.

Lowell Whiteman was originally built for serious ski racers. Students study diligently in the fall and spring so that during the winter, they can travel around the world, competing. For students like Sadie, who are not ski racers, Lowell Whiteman has a travel program. Every April these students go to destinations around the world doing service work. Sadie feeds people on the streets of India with Mother Teresa's missionaries; she builds chicken coops to help families in Honduras and Guatemala; she explores Bhutan; she works at a school in Thailand for girls at risk of being sold into the sex trade.

When Sadie goes to these faraway places, I reflect upon my own travels. Worry starts to creep in, then is replaced by the trust that, just as I grew through my experiences overseas, so will she.

The leader in Sadie emerges again, as she embraces school and inspires those around her by becoming class president in her senior year.

When it's time for graduation, Eric and I drive out to Steamboat. My dad and my aunt Judith fly in, too, and we all take our seats near the front. Sitting next to Judith, I'm reminded of how she showed up in my childhood. Mom's young sister was my idol. With her long blonde hair and blue eyes, I always thought she should be my sister rather than Mom's. She was so confident, though very volatile back then. Now she is serene and wise. How did she make this change? I want to be like her.

In her short, white lace dress and green Doc Martens, Sadie walks across the Lowell Whiteman School commencement stage to accept her first award. The "Ranking Scholar" award is given to the student in all grades, 9 through 12, with the highest academic grade point average for the year in a full-course load. She beams in surprise as her name is called to take the stage a second time to receive the "Head of School" award for leadership. Finally, she joins her 21 senior classmates to receive diplomas.

Judith and I are tearful, while Eric and Dad barely hold it together. *Thank God she made it!*

For college, Sadie attends the Moscow campus of the University of Idaho, in the northern part of the state. She studies outdoor leadership and psychology. During the summer, she's a river guide for a company on the Middle Fork of the Salmon River in Idaho, taking guests for six-day trips down 100 miles of rugged rapids, deep in the wilderness. She says it's the best therapy for her and the guests.

Sadie graduates in the spring of 2015, magna cum laude, and spends her summer guiding on the river. In the fall, she takes a job at the B-C Ranch on the border of the Frank Church–River of No Return Wilderness, overseeing a hunting lodge. People come from all over the world to hunt deer, elk, bear, and mountain lion.

Just after the New Year, a single guest arrives at the lodge, a man from the East Coast. He's determined to take home a prize, and already has the mount built for his trophy. He and Ron Ins, the lead guide and owner of the ranch, go out every day for five days, but come back empty-handed. The sixth and final day of hunting, Sadie is asked to join them.

When I see her next, Sadie recaps the events of the day. "Ron and the guest were on horses, with me bringing up the rear on a mule. We spent all day tracking. Finally, the hounds picked up a scent and bolted ahead, barking up a storm. It was really exciting as we ran through the woods. The idea is for the hounds to tree the mountain lion so the hunter can shoot it. We ran for a long time, and suddenly the barking of the dogs got closer. I thought they must have treed the animal. My adrenalin was racing."

"Sounds ghastly," I say.

"Oh Mama, it was incredible. The horses labored as we rode uphill through the trees. Getting closer to the sound of the hounds, I saw the blue skyline peek out from the top of the forest. As the sky grew bigger, I figured the mountain lion must be in a tree at the peak.

"As we rode higher and higher, we could see more. There were creeks and places I had never seen from above. I looked down at this landscape that has become my home, my place. We crested the hill to see the hounds frantically barking down the other side into the ravine. The mountain lion got away, and the hunter was furious."

I, however, am relieved to hear the big cat ran free.

Sadie continues, "On the way back, we crossed a wide creek. Ron went first, then the guest. It was 12 degrees, so the ice was pretty solid. The horses picked their steps carefully. My mule stepped on the ice and suddenly plummeted into the freezing cold water at a deep spot.

"The next thing I knew, I was submerged in the water and the mule was still under me. When I came to the surface, Ron said, 'It's time to get off the mule.' I swam, pushing broken ice out of my way to the shore. If I had been carried down the stream even 10 feet, I would have been sucked below the ice. I would have been a goner, since there was a thick layer of at least 100 yards of solid ice resting on top of the flowing water. The mule ended up making its way to the bank of the creek. We hightailed it back to the trailer to avoid hypothermia. Fortunately, we were only five miles from the lodge. I've never been so cold in my life!

"Who I am today, Mama, has so much to do with outdoor exploration. My times in the wilderness started it and these opportunities continue it."

The following summer, Sadie is excited to be back with her river company, guiding on the Middle Fork. She meets and falls in love with

Blake King, a fellow guide. Blake is tall, strong and handsome. Like Sadie, he believes in eating healthy, organic food. Living in the wilderness is a priority for them both.

Together, they take guests down the River of No Return. In the fall and winter, they work at various hunting lodges in the Frank Church Wilderness. During the off-season, they travel around the world.

"We're closing on a property on July 13th, Sue-Sue's birthday!" Sadie exclaims on the phone one day, in between river trips. They'll live in eastern Idaho next to a creek, a cottonwood grove, and a small apple orchard. Their goal is to be fully sustainable by planting more fruit trees, growing organic vegetables, tending animals, and constructing greenhouses for winter gardening.

In spite of all the hardships, but more likely because of them, Sadie has grown into an astonishing young woman.

Chapter 24

Tennis

When Raleigh is 12 years old, he discovers a love of tennis. "Mom, I'm going to play in the tournament at the park this weekend."

Eric and I are surprised, because we don't play tennis.

The weekend arrives, and I'm on the sidelines watching the match. I overhear some local boys talking. "I'm playing against Raleigh next. It'll be an easy win."

It's a close match with lots of cheering and excitement—but Raleigh wins. He goes on to defeat the next boy, and the next, winning first place.

"Mom, can you take me to the Gatorade Tennis Tournament in Boise next week?"

"Absolutely!"

The rest of the summer is filled with trips to Boise, the only city in Idaho big enough for real tennis competition. I savor the closeness and the time with my son.

Nearing the end of middle school and into his first year of high school, Raleigh is getting bored with his classes. A friend tells us about a new local private school—The Sage School—and suggests we check it out. Harry Weekes, a local teacher and innovator, has come up with the idea for a new kind of learning environment. We think it might give Raleigh more of a challenge.

The Sage School has an open house for prospective families in mid-August. We are excited to see Harry's plan to challenge students academically, according to their personal ability. Lots of time outdoors. Weekly volunteer opportunities in the community that give students a chance to experience the satisfaction of serving others. When the presentation is over, Raleigh asks, "Could I really go here?"

Raleigh attends Sage when they open in the fall. We're thrilled to discover that he can continue to play on the tennis team at the local high school. When he's on the sidelines, he sits with the tennis coach, Vicki, and helps her critique the players. He has a keen eye. "Raleigh is spot on when it comes to coaching," Vicki tells me later. "I appreciate his insights."

Freshman year, Raleigh qualifies for the state championship. Sophomore year, he and his doubles partner, Charlie, stun everyone by coming home with first place, and leading the school to its first-ever state championship at this level. After a disappointing third place at state his junior year, he and Charlie wrap up their senior year by winning state again. Watching my son work hard, push through and triumph, makes me feel successful, too.

Raleigh applies to only one college, Boise State University. It's close to home and has a nationally ranked tennis team. Three semesters in, Raleigh calls with eagerness in his voice. "Mom, there's a school in Michigan called Ferris State University that has a degree in professional tennis management. It's a four-year program with a hundred percent placement upon graduation. The coach says he might let me walk onto the team."

There are tennis facilities all over the world, but few places that train people to run them. Graduates of this program are in high demand. Raleigh is following his passion. We tell him to go for it. He flies out to begin winter semester.

By the following fall, Raleigh is ready to have his car at school. He and I drive from Sun Valley, Idaho, to Big Rapids, Michigan. It's my first time there, and I'm happy to see this quaint town and picturesque college. By visiting in person, I realize first-hand that Raleigh fits right in—he has found his tribe. The tennis team is made up of young men from all over the world: Indonesia, Russia, England, Spain, Germany, Canada, Australia, South Africa, Brazil, and Jamaica. In his own way, Raleigh is discovering his path in the same spirit as I did—he's thriving with different people, from all over the world, staying active and free.

Raleigh's enthusiasm shines as the men's tennis team makes it to nationals. They win conference for the first time in 20 years. They go on to make the round of 32 at the national tournament. The following year the team makes the final four at nationals, the furthest Ferris State's tennis team has ever gone. Raleigh's senior year, the team makes it to the elite eight at nationals.

Raleigh excels academically, too. His crowning achievement comes on the final certification exam, a comprehensive series of seven tests covering all aspects of tennis and coaching. In order to achieve the highest certification rating on the test, an applicant must receive "Elite" in all seven sections. Under the current format, no one has ever achieved it on his or her first attempt in the history of the United States Professional Tennis Association. Except Raleigh.

In 2017, he graduates magna cum laude. I simply could not be prouder.

Chapter 25

Manifesting

Back in 2008, when Sadie and Raleigh are each in a private high school, I'm struggling financially. Both kids are being challenged at their academic level, and this brings them contentment and happiness, which in turn brings me contentment and happiness. For me, however, paying half the tuition is becoming difficult. My home equity line of credit and my credit card debt run deep, and I'm still focusing a tremendous amount of energy on developing Nardagani, with the continued hope of finding Jay. I feel as though I'm in cruise mode, maintaining focus on Nardagani while my drug and alcohol use stays just inside my control. But I need income and I need rest.

At my spiritual center, Light on the Mountains, I learn a new way to experience my thinking. While I was growing up, my father, being a neurosurgeon, would say that when the body dies, so does the brain. That's it, the game of life is over. But Mom felt there was something more; she was agnostic.

One of my first friends growing up was Debbie; we met in junior high school. She exposed me to religion by taking me to her youth group, which was connected to her church. I loved being with the kids; they were accepting and warm. But the first time I joined Debbie and her family on Sunday at church, the message was that if you didn't believe in God, you'd burn in Hell. This got me worried.

At the end of the sermon, I spoke with the priest. "My father is a doctor, he saves people's lives. He's a good man, but he doesn't believe in God."

The priest's reply was simple. "He will burn in Hell."

"Oh, I see," I said thoughtfully. Looking up into the eyes of this tall man, I wonder: *what would God say?*

I didn't go near a church for many years, until I went to Light on the Mountains. I was 33, searching for guidance and a community of like-minded people. Upon entering the modest space where the service was held, peace filled my body, mind, and spirit. I had found my tribe.

One of the many things Reverend John teaches is to ask the Universe for what we want. His intention is to encourage contemplation on what it is we are seeking through our desires, like peace or joy. But I take it literally. So, one day, when I'm feeling desperate, I give it a try by hollering, "Okay God, I want a job where I can get paid to sleep!" And, miraculously, it works.

Three days later, I get a call from my friend Jen who does caregiving for private individuals. "Hey Narda, would you be interested in being on a caregiving team? Sadly, one of our clients is dying of cancer. We're looking for someone to work the night shift."

The next afternoon I go for an interview. Mary, a gracious, active member of our community, answers the door and leads me into her living room. She says she'll let her husband, Harold, know I'm here. She walks away, down a short hall. Suddenly, I hear a man's voice boom, "I don't need another damn caregiver!"

Mary pokes her head out and says, "He's ready to meet you."

Standing at the entrance of the bedroom, I fidget. An old man is lying in bed grumbling to himself. The room smells of flowers. I see a lovely bouquet of yellow roses on the dresser. The man raises his head, sees me, and a look of surprise lights up his face. "You're the woman who wrote that book with the symbols. Come over here. I have some questions."

As I sit in a chair next to the bed, Harold is already asking how my program works for people with dyslexia. We become fast friends.

Being in this lovely home four nights a week is delightful. In the living room, there is a big comfy couch where I sleep. A baby monitor is on the table nearby. Harold hardly ever needs me during the night. Around 10 p.m. each evening, I snuggle between the sheets, rest my head back on the pillow, and thank God for answering my prayers.

Four months later, Harold is becoming weak. He's nearing the end of his life. Caregivers are dropping off like flies, so I take on more shifts. The dying process fascinates me. There are many ways to go—slowly, like Harold, or fast, like Mom, who was here one day and gone the next.

Is Mom in heaven watching over me? Sometimes I sense she's here—a brush along my shoulder, or the random sound of a bell catches my attention from across the room. I've learned about Angel Numerology, which gives meaning to the numbers that repeat in our lives as signs from above. These days I see 777's a lot, which basically means, "Keep up the good work." I'm intrigued by it; the numbers give me comfort. *Thanks, Mom!*

Early one morning, I'm at home when I get a call from Mary. "Harold passed away during the night. Now's the time to pay last respects if you'd like to come by." It's the first time I have been physically close to a deceased person. A few candles are lit and the sensation is dreamlike. Harold looks so peaceful, as though he is sleeping. *When will I join you, Harold?* Although I knew him only a short time, my connection with him felt like it was meant to be. We came into each other's lives, however fleeting, at just the right time. I'll miss him.

It's time to find another job. At a loss for how to begin the search, I wonder if the Universe is still receptive. So I shout out, "Okay God, I'd like a job where I get paid to hike with my dog."

Sadie and Raleigh had talked me into getting Rocco years ago. I remember their persuasiveness: "Please Mom, we'll do anything!"

"Find a puppy that's mellow and doesn't shed, and I'll consider it." *Good luck!*

A few days later, the kids rushed in the front door after school, shouting, "Mom, we found him! He's part of a litter from the animal shelter. The mom and her pups are staying at Ellen's house up the street. Come see!"

Sure enough, there was one shorthaired pup lying down in the grass. All the other black and white fur balls were running around the yard, hopping, licking, and falling over themselves. Picking up Rocco, I found he was mush in my hands. He just stared at me with his big black eyes. I, too, became mush.

At this point, Sadie is away at high school in Colorado and Raleigh has made the decision to live full time with Eric instead of continuing to move back and forth every week. Raleigh never liked moving from my house to Eric's. It was chaotic. So, walking Rocco falls on me, three times a day. I've never felt more alone in my life. But each day I get up, get dressed, and oblige my furry dependent by taking him on his walks. I'm moving my feet for Rocco, in the direction of teaching people to read—and bringing Jay home.

Within a couple of days, I get a call from a man named Henry. His wife, Claire, has a rare disease, a form of aphasia. She's physically fit, but has lost the ability to speak. He tells me they communicate through writing, though she's losing that faculty as well. L.A. is their home and they're renting a house in the Sun Valley area for the summer.

"Would you take Claire and our dog hiking?"

"Can I bring my dog, too?"

"Of course."

Claire appears to be happy when she's outdoors. We hike all over the mountains around the Wood River Valley. When I arrive to pick her up, I ask where she wants to hike and she carefully scrawls a location on a piece of paper. But within a month, she can no longer write. In her frustration, she writes the same letter over and over, "s ... s ... s ... s" as tears spill from her eyes. Taking charge, I say, "Let's go on one of my favorite hikes."

Sometimes we hike in silence and other times I talk, never asking questions, only sharing stories. I talk about my life and about Jay. My habit of always searching for Jay when I'm hiking is never-ending. My eyes are always open, determined not to accidentally walk right by the answer. *Could he be in the bushes just off this trail?* Looking down, I notice a heart-shaped rock on the path. I show it to Claire and her smile grows wide. Finding heart rocks becomes our quest. We each have a nice collection by the time summer is over and Claire goes back to L.A.

Winter is coming. What will my next job be? I would love to be on the mountain skiing and snowboarding, something I haven't done in several years because of the expense. A few years back, I worked for Sun Valley Company teaching snowboarding. I got a free pass, but waiting around without pay for the next student made me anxious.

"God, I'd love to get paid to ski, but not have to teach."

The next morning an email comes in from Henry. He wants to hire me to take Claire skiing. He's planning to rent a condo and they'll travel to Sun Valley regularly throughout the ski season. He buys me a season's pass. Our first day on the slopes, I see that Claire is a beautiful skier. We spend many days swooshing down the slopes. After skiing, we enjoy après-ski at the bottom of the mountain on the deck. Claire laughs easily, though no sound comes out of her mouth.

As the ski season winds down, Claire comes to town for the last weekend the mountain is open. We enjoy spring skiing. Spring snow is called 'corn snow'—crunchy and slushy under our skis, falling aside as we make our turns. After the street party at the base of Bald Mountain, Claire and I say goodbye with a long hug. I feel fulfilled having brought joy to her simple life over these many months.

Spring is typically rainy here in the mountains. I stay indoors, without my usual motivation to don a rain jacket and get some exercise. Without a TV, I find short videos and interviews to watch on my computer. One day I see a woman talking about weight loss. As I've always struggled with those few extra pounds, I pay attention to her new technique. She simply visualizes her body just how she wants it to be, while she is moving through her day, showering, lying in bed on her way to sleep. That's it.

It's harder than it sounds, but I make this visualization my habit. I picture my body svelte and strong—in the shower, when I wake, when I go to bed every night, and whenever I walk, chanting as I strut tall. "I am love, I am light, my body is fit, my tummy is tight!"

It works. My body is thinning. I am becoming what I visualize.

That spring I meet Roxanne at Light on the Mountains. She approaches me in the social hall after service. "I hear you're a caregiver."

"For about a year now. I don't have any formal training. I'm an artist, actually."

"My significant other is dying of cancer. I want someone to help me a couple nights a week. I'm so tired, I need some sleep."

I stay with Roxanne and Bill three nights a week. It's a small condo and we decide Roxanne will sleep in the spare room and I'll sleep in the king bed with Bill. It's less strange than it sounds—he needs support, and my time with him is Roxanne's time to get some shuteye.

I'm a very quiet, solid sleeper. It's not a big deal for me to sleep on the far side of the huge bed while Bill sleeps on the other side. When he needs me in the night, he simply reaches over and taps me on the shoulder.

Two months later, Bill dies. My friendship with Roxanne grows deep as we get together often. She is a 74-year-old woman with light red hair. Her robust sense of humor makes whole congregations erupt with laughter. With a twinkle in her eye, Roxanne likes to introduce me as the woman who slept with her husband.

I love that with Bill, Harold, and their partners, I've had the privilege of walking with these souls at their most intimate moments, to make these sad times a little more bearable when I can.

I continue to get odd jobs while I work on Nardagani. One day it's clear to me that my mortgage payment is fine for a successful real estate agent, but too high for a person with my current income, and my home equity line of credit is nearly maxed out. I call my lender and tell her that I can't make the mortgage payments. I stop writing the monthly mortgage check and list my house for sale. A couple of months later, I arrive home to an orange note on my door—I'm officially in foreclosure. Fortunately, several weeks after that, I secure a buyer. When the sales contract is solid, I pack what I need and move into the small room at Roxanne's condo. She's a delightful roommate and host.

Instead of stewing in worry, I see the situation for what it is: a pivotal point in my life. I've gone from homeowner to couch surfing. Instead of renting a storage unit, I decide it's time to let go. Two weekends in a row I have garage sales at my lovely home, which will no longer be mine in three weeks.

People hand me money and walk away with all my belongings— my furniture, everything in my kitchen, much of my clothing, treasures that had been Mom's, and my car. Eric graciously takes Rocco. It's a purging of physical things, and I simply feel lighter. Sometimes I realize that starting over means peeling back the layers. It means forcing myself to do the hard thing—what had previously seemed impossible.

For seven months I stay with Roxanne. I use a small table in my space as a desk. I walk or take the bus to odd jobs around town. I like being a minimalist. Life is simple.

In my post office box one day, there's a letter from Mary. She thanks me for being a blessing in her life and says that Harold's affairs are finally settled. They want me to have this gift. I look in the envelope and find a check. It's enough money to rent a small apartment for a while, and buy a modest vehicle. I'm astounded by her generosity.

An unfurnished condo is available for rent on the east side of Ketchum. Friends offer an assortment of items to help fill the empty spaces—a bed, a couch, a table, and four chairs. I purchase some kitchen items and bedding at the local thrift store to complete my home. Rocco returns. My life is fairly calm and quiet. The rebuilding has begun.

One day while deep-cleaning the condo, I notice the windows are filthy. I clean them on the inside, but I'm two stories up, so the exterior is higher than I can reach. I call around to several window-cleaning companies. A man named Larry, whom I know from around town, returns my call. "It's busy because of all the rain we had the last few weeks. Everyone wants their windows done."

"Well, could you lend me a ladder so I can wash them myself?"

"I'll lend you a ladder and all the tools if you'll work for me until I get caught up. I'll teach you to wash windows on your windows first." I'm surprised by his offer, but thankful for this new opportunity.

The next morning, Larry secures a belt around my waist. Hanging from the belt is a long, narrow bucket of soapy water, scrubbers and squeegees. He's a good teacher, and within an hour I'm clicking along at a nice rhythm. I like the hard, physical work of moving the tall ladders, climbing up and down, and leaving every window sparkling.

Three weeks later, when all his accounts are clean, Larry is ready to get back to his solo gig.

"But I want to keep going," I say to him.

"There are plenty of windows to go around," he replies.

After purchasing ladders and the gear, and securing insurance, I tell all my friends there's a new professional window washer in town.

By day, I wash windows, hiring Jen and my friend Roni to help with big jobs. By night, I work on Nardagani. It all looks good on the outside, but on the inside my heart is heavy, and depression lurks. Nightmares of Jay suffering continue to haunt me. I wake up with my eyes shut tight, hoping the day will not come.

I have a growing awareness that I need help to dig my way out of this depression. Therapy works when I have the funds, so I look for a program through social services. After an interview, I'm allotted six free therapy sessions. But that's not enough.

I feel like everything has caught up with me. Despite trying to let go, my use of alcohol and marijuana increases, temporarily distracting me from the depression. A puff gets me moving every morning. Every few hours I look for my next lift. In the afternoon, I anxiously check my watch, waiting for the hour when it's okay to pour my first glass of wine. Sometimes I have a shot of tequila to get me through the day. The relief is only temporary. I'm not who I want to be. I remember standing on the top of the world with Sadie in the wilderness three years ago. The book she read by Viktor Frankl reminds me of her words, "We must rehabilitate our thinking."

My neighbor, Mary Austin Crofts, tells me about Eye Movement Desensitization and Reprogramming (EMDR), a rapid eye movement therapy. I go to the local clinic and they're able to pay for me to have six sessions. During the treatments, a feeling of peace eases my mind. The therapist teaches me to feel resilient with each bad day. But again, the mere six appointments leave me wanting more.

One afternoon, at the post office, a friend pulls me aside. She senses my dis-ease. "I'm on my way to a 12-step recovery meeting. Why don't you come with me?"

Maybe this is an invitation from Mom. I go to the meeting. The people are warm and welcoming. I share my story and feel connected. The only requirement for joining is a desire to stop drinking.

That's me.

There are so many meetings offered that it's easy for me to make time to go to at least one every day. I find a sponsor who takes me through the 12 Steps. Going through the steps requires a lot of reading and homework, and it takes me nearly a year to complete. I've never had such a thorough look at myself. For the first time, I am getting a glimpse of who I am.

I'm a person who grew up in a dysfunctional home. My beliefs about the world were formed a long time ago, and they're wrong. People can be trusted. I am lovable. And my feelings matter.

The tools for living a life of intention and clarity are abundant. I feel renewed, refreshed.

Chapter 26

A New Friend

Rhet and I first meet in 2006, when we arrive at the same moment at my neighbor's home for a birthday party. As I saunter down their long driveway, a motorcycle rumbles in behind me. Turning to watch it approach, I step aside as the Harley slows and coasts by. The rider has wavy brown hair sticking out from under his helmet. Behind his round glasses, I see his eyes on me. He stops the bike and fumbles to put the kickstand down. The bike wobbles and nearly drops. Finally securing it, he jumps off and runs over.

"Hi, I'm Rhet. May I walk in with you?"

He's tall and muscular. On his lean frame, his features are large: nose, ears, hands, and feet. Enormous toes protrude from his Birkenstocks. Rhet's eyes are sky blue with eyelids that droop low, especially at the outside corners. *Who is this adorable guy?*

Side by side we walk toward the house. A high vibration buzzes in my head as his arm brushes my shoulder. He opens the door for me with one hand and takes my elbow with the other. The feeling is electric. Once inside the house, Rhet follows close behind as I head to the kitchen. I've brought everyone's favorite appetizer, which I learned to make with my mom in Japan. Setting down my platter of sushi on the counter, I give our hostess, Margie, a hug, then turn and head out the back door.

The Big Wood River flows by within a hundred yards of the deck. The river is full and strong—breathtaking, actually, with cottonwood trees standing tall and powerful at its edge, and the mountain jutting up sharply on the opposite bank. The sound of the flowing water is enchanting. It's a perfect spring afternoon, not a cloud in the piercing blue sky, warm with a hint of fresh breeze coming off the water.

Rhet has a deep, soothing voice. "Let's get a drink. I can't leave your side." He reaches out for my hand. I don't take it, but say "Sure," and walk toward a table on the lawn with bottles of wine and Perrier.

"I'll have a Perrier, please," I say. After we get our drinks, Rhet coaxes me to join him on a bench next to the water's edge. We sit on soft cushions. "Tell me everything about yourself," he says.

"No, you start."

Rhet tells me about how he grew up in the Bahamas and, as a boy, hunted in the sea. Every fall the water grew black with lobsters. He'd dive down and gather four or five at a time on his homemade spear gun, called a sling. Sometimes, they had so many in the freezer that his mom would punish him by making him eat lobster for breakfast, lunch, and dinner.

"Mom was an early member of the Rockettes in New York. She had access to all kinds of exotic people. She used to invite Ram Dass to dinner on a regular basis. Though she wasn't a calm person herself, she raised us kids with the daily practice of yoga and meditation."

I was loving Rhet's story, and was impressed that he knew the well-known spiritual guru.

Influenced by Ram Dass, Rhet took to yoga and meditation. Rhet's three siblings teased him—every night at 7 p.m., he made tea and went to his bedroom. He found calm in a world of chaos.

His father traveled throughout the islands of the Bahamas installing satellite tracking stations for NASA. Sometimes Rhet joined his dad in remote places, and tutors were flown in for schooling.

"In the late sixties, our family moved to Florida. It was crowded and noisy in Palm Beach. My parents weren't getting along. At 16, I ran away from home. Some hippie friends and I had just seen the movie

Jeremiah Johnson. We were inspired to go to the mountains and homestead some land. Three of us piled into a VW bug with all the gear we could imagine we would need. We were quite the picture. When we were out of room inside the car, we tied shovels and picks to the outside with rope. Squeezing into the bug, our mantra was, 'Go West, young man.' We were attracted to Idaho because the population was decreasing. When we arrived in Salmon, Idaho, it was springtime."

"What about your mom? You called her, right?"

"I was a bad teenager, off on my own trip. We hooked up with a mountain man named Dick Zimmerman. He dug caves in the side of a mountain where he lived. One cave was so deep he hit ice, and that became his freezer. They called him Dugout Dick. I rented a cave from him for five dollars a month. He taught me to dry-stack stone, and I've been a stonemason ever since."

"But what about your mom?"

"Well, a couple of years later, I was traveling on my Harley across Canada when I was stopped by a 'Mounty' for speeding. He gave me a warning. As he got back into his vehicle, an alert came up on his radio that said I was a missing person and I needed to call my mother immediately."

When Rhet finally did call his mother, she begged him to go to a college she'd picked out for him: Maharishi International University (MIU) in Fairfield, Iowa. MIU offers a consciousness-based education. The dress code was three-piece suits, and Rhet had one for every day of the week. Students meditated in large groups, often several thousand at a time. During one event, people came from all over the world; the organizers counted over 10,000 meditators.

With my limited exposure to meditation, I'm fascinated and want to know more.

At that time, in 1975, honorary educators from around the world came to teach at MIU. Hans Salié taught psychology; Lawrence Domash, Ph.D., a Nobel Laureate, presented classes in physics; Robert Bly, the world-renowned poet and author of *Iron John: A Book About Men*, taught a semester course in philosophy. According to Rhet, Bly was very theatrical—he would come into the classroom every day wearing an outlandish mask to point out to the students that we all tend to wear masks, until we become aware that we're wearing them. Bly quoted poetry by Rumi and all the masters with great animation.

To help pay his tuition, Rhet worked in the kitchen and became a superb cook.

He graduated with a degree in interdisciplinary studies and then reignited his passion for stone masonry. He had job opportunities on the East Coast, where his natural artistic abilities caught the attention of top designers like Versace and Estée Lauder. He got to work with movie stars all around the world, embellishing their homes with marble columns and Greek mosaics.

Rhet's stories grip me. I want to sit there all evening and listen to him, but friends come over to say hello and encourage us to get some food. With heaping plates, we find two seats at a table by the river. His tales continue.

Breaking my trance, I notice everyone is gathering on the porch to sing "Happy Birthday" to Cameron, our host. I'm delighted to sing the new take I've heard on the Happy Birthday song: "Happy birthday, happy birthday, we love you. Happy birthday, happy birthday, may all your dreams come true. When you blow out the candles, one light stays aglow. That's the love light in your eyes wherever you go."

Cake is being served on bone china. I take a piece and walk away from the crowd. Wandering around the side of the house, I find there is a lovely creek that feeds the river.

"How about some tea with your cake?" The deep voice is Rhet's. He is carrying a small tray with his cake, two cups of steaming tea and a lit candle. "Come sit with me," he beckons. I follow him to a small table next to the creek. The cushions are comfy. "Your turn to talk," he says.

I believe that to share is to heal. *Oh, how I want to heal.* Telling the short version of my story brings Rhet to the edge of his seat. A while later, I look up to see nearly everyone else has gone inside. The moon is reflected in the flowing water of the creek. Rhet asks for my phone number. I need to be honest. "My kids are young, only in middle school.

They're my focus. Also, I'm not a good girlfriend. Jay's disappearance and my mom's death messed up my head *and* my heart."

After that night, Rhet and I become friends. We see each other at parties, around town, and up skiing. Being in relationship is intriguing, but I know that I'm happy alone right now. Life is simpler. My kids and my friends fill me with love. My passions are finding Jay and creating Nardagani. I don't need anything else.

Chapter 27

Falling

"Rowan fell off the ladder! He's lying on the pavers in a pool of blood!!" It's my friend, Roni, screaming through my cell phone.

I can hear people shouting in the background: "Someone call 911!"

My heart jolts. I can't breathe. Roni and Rowan, my two assistants, said they could handle the window washing job without me. Beads of sweat break out on my neck. Roni is babbling, though I hear her say "drunk" and "beer cans in his car," as the sound of a siren grows loud. Click. The phone goes dead.

I'm in my car parked outside my attorney's office in Boise, a three-hour drive from Ketchum, where Roni and Rowan are. I'm here to talk about securing a copyright for the Nardagani Reading Program. My mind flashes back to this morning when I spoke with Rowan. A rapid fire of thoughts fills my mind. *Oh my God, could he be dead?*

Rowan is an alcoholic. Two years earlier, when I met him at one of my first recovery meetings, he was charming. He had a captivating sparkle in his light blue eyes and a slanted, quirky smile. He is about 5 feet 10 inches tall with curly grey hair poking out from under a baseball cap. There was something about him that enchanted me. He had been the favorite local pharmacist for many years in our small community. He was knowledgeable and kind—he charmed everyone.

One day at work, he was accused of stealing pills. When Rowan admitted his fault, said he would quit being a pharmacist and go to recovery meetings, his employers agreed not to press charges. His pharmaceutical license was revoked, and Rowan went on to become a full-time ski instructor for Sun Valley Company in the winter and a wrencher (someone who works on bicycles) in the summer.

"Hey, how about going for a drink?" he asked me after the meeting. "Ha-ha, a Shirley Temple and Roy Rogers, of course."

A fleeting concern made me pause, but I joined him anyway.

Because of his background in pharmaceuticals and decades of experience in recovery, Rowan had a vast knowledge of drugs and alcohol. For me, the disease was still perplexing. Both Jay and Mom were gone because of their inability to stay sober. At one point, as we were getting to know each other, I asked Rowan, "Why can't an alcoholic just stop drinking?" We spent time mulling it over, comparing theories and stories from our lives.

Being in recovery is good for me. I've stopped drinking, though I decide to quit just one vice at a time. Marijuana is medicinal, right? Ever so slowly, I begin to understand why Mom and Jay struggled with sobriety. I'm learning that alcoholism is a disease, not a choice.

One morning, Rowan doesn't show up at the 12-step meeting. He doesn't answer his phone. I stop by his apartment and knock on his door ... nothing. For two days I hear nothing from him. A disconcertingly familiar, uncomfortable worry begins to grow in me. *Where is he?*

Just as my stomach begins to tighten and my body starts to tremble with fear, a moment of clarity comes to me. This is the habit of my body and my mind when I'm searching for something or someone.

Stop! Breathe! Trust all will be well! I repeat this to myself over and over, but peace is just beyond my grasp.

On the third morning, Rowan's friend, Michael, approaches me after the meeting and says, "Would you like to ride with me out to his apartment? He probably relapsed."

"But he wasn't there yesterday."

"He's there," Michael says, as we get into his white Subaru.

We arrive at Rowan's apartment and knock on the door. No answer. Michael finds the apartment manager and gets a key. When Michael opens the door, the smell of cigar smoke hits my nostrils. I back out into the hallway to collect myself. My second time entering, the stench of stale beer is intense. Rowan is in his bed, beer cans all over the floor and piled up in the corner of his small kitchen in an overflowing garbage bin.

Michael sighs—he's seen this before. "Let's take him to the hospital. He needs an IV with fluids."

Together, we help Rowan up and walk him out to Michael's car. I climb into the back seat and we drive off.

At the hospital, Rowan is put in a bed surrounded by a white curtain. Michael and I sit on hard plastic chairs in the corner. The antiseptic smell seeps into my nose and throat. An IV is stuck in Rowan's arm. Slowly, he becomes more conscious. The curtain is drawn back to reveal a tall man in a white smock and pants. "Hi Rowan, back again? We can't keep you here. You'll get fluids, then you need to be on your way."

Unexpectedly, Rowan rips the IV out of his arm, pushes the doctor out of the way, climbs off the bed and walks with determination down the hall, through the door and out into the parking lot. "Take me home!" he orders Michael, vehemently, when we catch up to him.

We load up in Michael's car and drive down the road.

"I don't understand," I say to Michael.

"We made it clear to Rowan the last time he relapsed that nobody would take him in again. We're done."

I can't believe what I'm hearing. "You mean, we just take him back to his place ... to die?"

Michael breathes deeply. "Yes."

"This is crazy. I'll take a turn. Go right at the light; my apartment is on the left."

Once we arrive home and Rowan is settled on my couch, I bring him tea.

"Narda, I need to tell you something," Rowan says, hesitating. "I was completely sober for almost a decade. But then, six years ago, a beautiful woman, Vera, walked into a meeting. She was new in town. She'd moved here from the East Coast, where she had been sober for many years. She signed up for ski lessons, and I was her instructor. Several lessons along, we started dating and then fell in love. We were together a year when Vera decided she could find a rich man in this affluent town. She left me and I relapsed."

After a long silence, he continues. "Six months later, Vera showed up at my door. I was so relieved. A few months after that, she left again. I relapsed again. She left me two more times."

We talk into the night about how alcoholism makes a mess of people's lives. Rowan tells me that he hasn't been able to stop relapsing, and the time between his relapses continues to shrink. Recently, a psychiatrist gave him a book called *The End of My Addiction*, whose author, Olivier Ameisen, M.D., writes about using a drug called Baclofen to stop the cravings for alcohol. The psychiatrist knew Rowan had been a pharmacist and said he would write him a prescription for anything he wanted to try. Baclofen, in combination with Ativan, worked to reduce his cravings, but not completely. Rowan is hopeful that one day, when someone steps up with funding for research, there may be a cure for alcoholic cravings. Meanwhile, he's searching for a way to stay alive, with the disease of alcoholism coursing through his mind and body.

For five days, I nurse Rowan back to health. Then we return to our routine of morning meetings and mountain biking. My feelings for Rowan are growing. Nursing him back to health and our long conversations have fueled a deep connection between us.

Sitting on the grass beside the trail one day, enjoying a sandwich, he looks into my eyes and says, "I'm in love with you."

"I'm in love with you, too." Within a couple of months, Rowan moves in with me.

The ringing of the phone startles me. It's Roni again. "He's alive, Narda. They're transporting him by helicopter to Saint Alphonsus Hospital in Boise."

We share the silence as a surreal fog wraps around my mind.

Roni begins talking through sobs. "Narda … I'm so sorry to tell you … but … I smelled alcohol on Rowan's breath earlier. I went to get a tool out of the back of his car and saw several empty beer cans."

So, that's why he fell off the ladder.

"Thanks for telling me, Roni. I'm late for my appointment."

I take a moment to compose myself, then open my car door and head into the building. The attorney begins the copyright and trademark process.

As soon as the meeting ends, I go to St. Al's Hospital. Rowan is still in surgery, so I try to get comfortable in the waiting room. He's in there for hours. Growing restless, I pace, then walk to the cafeteria and buy nothing. I walk around the grounds of the large building, then back to the waiting room, then up and down the halls. *What a mess. Will he be okay?*

It's 10 p.m. when I feel a hand gently shake my shoulder. Opening my eyes, I look up to see the doctor.

"We've done all we can. Come with me."

We walk down the hall and into a room with a computer monitor on the wall. "This is a CAT scan of Rowan's brain. See this area here?"

As he shows me the parts of the brain, I think of my father, the neurosurgeon, and the many stories he told at dinnertime. The doctor tells me that most likely Rowan is brain-dead. If, by some miracle, this is not the case, Rowan will never walk again or be able to speak or eat. A black cloud engulfs me. The doctor's lips continue to move, but the words jumble together and go over my head. When he's done talking, I leave the hospital and get a room at the hotel next door.

Since my relationship with Rowan began four years ago, I've watched him battle with sobriety. It appears he has lost. I love him, but I'm also ready to move forward and leave this struggle behind.

The next day I check in with the nurse. She tells me Rowan is in a coma. I wander the halls of the hospital in a daze, not sure what to do.

My phone rings. It's Rowan's brother, Clyde. "I'll be driving to Boise soon. My buddy, Charlie Brandt, will be with me. We're picking up our sister, JoAnne, at the airport. She's flying in from Portland. I'll let you know when we get to the hospital."

JoAnne, Clyde, and Charlie show up four hours later. They have a chance to look in on Rowan and talk with the doctor. We're not sure what to do, so we go to a nearby Thai restaurant for lunch. Together, we plan Rowan's funeral. Each of us will speak. They are okay with my desire to talk about Rowan's search for a cure.

After lunch, they drop me off at my car in the parking lot of the hospital. Clyde says, "Please go home and rest. We'll see you back in Ketchum."

I feel numb and shaky. I don't remember getting in my car or driving the three hours toward home. I'm in too much shock to cry, until, on my way through Hailey, I stop to see my friend Rhet, a gentle soul. He hugs me tightly as my tears flow.

He's heartbroken that I've fallen in love with Rowan. He's been dating women in town, but he moves from one to another, always searching for something deeper.

But I don't have time to think about Rhet now. I spend my days in a haze. I go through my usual routine: work, eat, sleep, and shop for food. Everywhere I go, people tell me they're praying for Rowan to recover.

Eleven days after his fall off the ladder, I'm at the gas station buying fuel. My bill is $55.55. It's Rowan's 55th birthday. That's a lot of fives, which means, in Angel Numerology, buckle your seatbelt, a major life change is upon you.

An hour later, my phone rings. It's the doctor. "Narda, Rowan woke up. It's astonishing. His eyes are tracking, his facial expressions vary. The brain damage is much less than we thought."

On my way back to Boise, I stop again to see Rhet in Hailey. "Rowan woke up! But I'm afraid he's never going to be able to walk or talk again."

Rhet gives me a big hug and sends me on my way. For the rest of the drive, I wonder how it will be, taking care of my mate who may not be able to care for himself in the most basic ways. Being the loyal person that I am, I envision taking care of an invalid for the rest of my life. What a burden. *Here we go.*

I knock softly on the door, then walk into Rowan's hospital room. He's sitting up in bed. His eyes grow wide when he sees me. Pulling a chair up close to him, I take his hand, "How are you?"

He tries to talk, then shakes his head slowly. We just sit and stare at each other. His eyes are bluer than I remember. He has a monstrous scar down the middle of his forehead. I notice his wrists are strapped down. When the nurse comes in, I ask her why.

"He won't stop picking at his stitches," she says.

The rest of the day, I sit with Rowan and share news of home. I'm overjoyed he's alive, but I can't stop staring at his grotesque wound and thinking about his lack of ability to speak. The next morning, Rowan is able to drink water. It's a miracle. The day after that, he insists on getting out of bed. He groans as he moves his legs off the bed and puts his feet on the floor. With help, he stands, then sits back down, then stands again. By late afternoon he's able to walk very slowly with a walker. On the fourth day, he's able to walk carefully around the whole ward. The doctor stops in to say Rowan is being transferred to the physical therapy wing of the hospital.

Gently, we get him into a wheelchair. Following the nurse, we go to a room at the far end of the hospital. Once he's settled in, it's time for me to go home for a few days. Rowan takes my hand and pulls me close. With tremendous effort he whispers in my ear, "thththaaaank oo."

For the next several weeks, I travel back and forth to Boise. Each time I'm there, Rowan is better. He can speak a few words at a time, with concerted effort. He begins to eat again and spends a couple of hours a day in rehab. In three months, Rowan is ready to go home.

Before leaving Boise, we go to the Thai restaurant down the street from the hospital. We're seated at the same table where I sat with Clyde, JoAnne, and Charlie planning Rowan's funeral.

Once back at the condo, Rowan navigates the stairs fairly well. Settling in, he continues the routine set up at the hospital: resting, physical exercises twice a day, and mental exercises on a computer game three times a day to help his memory.

We have a quiet life for three months. Rowan communicates mostly through writing, though he can speak a bit with determination. I'm overjoyed at his progress, but I know that our relationship has shifted. I feel more like a caregiver than a girlfriend. He writes that the desire to drink alcohol has been knocked out of his head. I realize we haven't gone to a meeting since before his fall.

Miraculously, Rowan begins biking. He's getting better, but I'm restless and agitated. This relationship is a drag on my energy, and I feel stuck as a caregiver when I want to be a girlfriend, an intimate mate. Sometimes the mean woman appears. She takes over my body and yells in anger. Poor Rowan, he's simply trying to recover from a fall that should have taken his life.

I'm still sober, but smoking marijuana seems to take the edge off, so I continue.

One day, completely out of left field, our friend Jazebel shows up in her baby blue Ford truck. She bounces into our living room. "Hi! Ready, Rowan?" She's a thin woman with a head of blonde curls, a real knockout. Rowan turns to me and says haltingly, "I ... I ... I ... go Jazzzzbelllll."

What's going on? I watch as she packs up Rowan's things into a few boxes. She then hoists them up on her shoulder, goes out and down the stairs.

"Okay Rowan, let's go," she calls up the stairs.

He turns to me and stutters, "Thhhhank ooooou."

Off they go, into the truck, down the road, and out of sight.

I plunk down on the couch, dumbfounded. I'm not sure how to feel. Our relationship had shifted after the accident, but Jazebel? Are they dating? When did this happen? I realize I must have been so checked out that he developed this relationship and planned to leave with her, all unbeknownst to me.

Oh Jay, where are you? I need to talk.

I pull out some weed and enjoy a long, slow draw. I'm high, and still confused. I look around my apartment and wonder, *What am I doing with my life, and why did I fall in love with Rowan, of all people?*

Within minutes, bewilderment turns to clarity. I had a strong desire to learn, on a very deep level, why the disease of alcoholism took Jay and Mom. I realize Rowan had physical cravings for alcohol, just as I have hunger and a need to eat. The only way for Jay and Mom to beat back these physical cravings was to have tremendous spiritual and emotional support, which they got through actively attending recovery meetings. When they didn't attend the meetings and have the support of the fellowship, they were no match for the disease. It was an unforgiving simplicity.

But I'm not ready to apply this knowledge to myself. A state of dis-ease, of fog, has crept in as I've drifted away from meetings and the support from my recovery group. This place of isolation is comfortable, but dangerous.

I walk down the street to the liquor store and buy a bottle of tequila, then return home to loneliness and pour myself a tequila and o.j. Now that Rowan has left me, I decide to take another long break from men.

Chapter 28

Apex

Whenever unidentified people turn up dead in the Northwest, I get a call.

"The body was found in a reservoir near Boise. We've sent it in for identification. There's not much to go on, except a belt. I'll email you a picture of the belt," says an officer.

Hanging up the phone, my heart sinks. *I'm strong now, I can do this.* But I feel panic sinking in, a tide of sensation coming on, and I let my emotions take over. I go to my most quiet place, my bed. Blinking fast doesn't hold back the tears. My body shakes out of control. I calm my nerves with a hit of weed.

When the picture arrives, it gets forwarded around to our family. We want it to be Jay's belt, so that we can mourn him at last, but we also don't want it to be his belt. In the end, we know that Jay would never wear this—it's colorful and woven.

Another day, a call comes in from an officer on the case at the Hailey Police Department. He tells me to go to a website for unidentified dead people, grimly named unidentifieddeadbodies.com. "Enter yesterday's date and the city, Kennewick, Washington," he says. "A man was found yesterday in the closet of a hotel room. He hanged himself. He looks like Jay."

In my hesitancy, I scroll slowly through the deceased individuals. The images are appallingly morbid. I think about the families who come to this website to look, like me, expecting to discover the whereabouts of loved ones, yet hoping they're not here. My eyes land on a man who looks like Jay. His eyes and neck are weirdly swollen, black and blue. The face is too thin. *Could Jay have lost weight?*

But no, the man's eyes are too close together.

Relief washes over me as I realize it can't be my brother. Pushing back in my chair, I gag into the trashcan under my desk.

That night, I dream that people are turning into skeletons and chasing me. If they catch me, I'll turn into a horrific skeleton like them. The dream goes on and on. I see people being caught and turned into corpses, and then I'm spotted. I run faster and faster. When my arm is grabbed hard from behind, knocking me to the ground, I wake in a tangle of sheets and blankets, my heart racing. I don't want to go back to sleep. I don't want another dream like that. But I'm so tired.

The next morning, I drag myself out of bed and think about Nardagani—how it might help others like Jay, others who have never managed to read at a literate level. I know how often the fate of struggling readers is fraught with challenges. If I can stop the pattern for even one person, one family, I should.

I gather my strength and get back to work. It's time to collect all my materials, the book I began writing long ago, with Raleigh's edits and Sadie's art, and dust them off. I give them to Blake Thornton, a graphic artist out of southern Idaho, and he gets to work. Blake lays out the book, places Sadie's drawings, and then creates his own delightful illustrations wherever there are empty spaces.

"I have a book to print," I say to the salesman at Northwest Printing in Boise. We're sitting in his conference room surrounded by books and all kinds of printed materials. He looks over my manuscript as I explain about Nardagani and the symbols.

"We can print this 8 by 10," he says. "A 55-page book in full color, with a pocket in the front to hold the Sound Map, for $9.11 per book if you order 2,000 of them."

It seems like a terrific price for full color. *I'm sure to have 2,000 students, right?* I'm sweating bullets as I give him the okay to print 2,000 books with the title, *Reading English the Nardagani Way.*

It's October 18, 2010, nine years since Jay's disappearance. Sadie and Raleigh are in college. I'm sitting in my home office. I've finally finished the huge task of adapting the Japanese system of learning to read for English. It works. It's easy for anyone to learn (a parent, friend, tutor or teacher) and simple to teach. I've gone completely out of my comfort zone, and I did it to find Jay.

I write an email to my Webmaster. "Thank you, Krissy, we did it! The website looks great! My newly printed books, coded with the Nardagani symbols, have arrived. I'm ready to launch this program out into the world. Thank you for all your wonderful work!"

Pushing back from my desk on my rolling chair, I take a deep breath, put my fists in the air and yell, "Okay God. I'm in huge debt. I've worked for nine years to finish this program. WHERE IS MY BROTHER?"

As I take my next breath, the phone rings. It's Sheriff Walt Femling. "Narda, please come to the sheriff's department. A hunter found some human remains out in East Fork."

Startled and in shock, I put the phone down carefully. The minutes of joy and celebration fade into dread. I sit for a spell, feeling numb. Then, I get in my car and drive to Femling's office, thinking the whole way, *It's not Jay. He's alive and well and will be coming home soon.*

I sit across the desk from the sheriff.

Femling is matter-of-fact. "A hunter found a human skull 1.7 miles out East Fork Road, up a canyon to the north. He was on his horse and saw something reflecting light from the sun. When he got closer, he saw that it was a skull. Our team went out to the area and collected the skull and some bones. There was nothing else, no clothing."

I'm starting to shake, barely able to hold on.

"But we searched there. It can't be Jay."

"The skull is being sent to Boise for identification. We'll match dental records."

"I want to see it! I know Jay's teeth!" But with a lump in my throat, I realize I'm afraid to see the skull.

"No. It's wrapped up, going to Boise in the morning. It shouldn't take long. I'll let you know."

Later that week, I'm shocked to see my face in the newspaper, my picture next to Jay's. Friends who see the article tell me, "You'll have closure now."

No, it isn't Jay. He's alive and coming home soon.

Friends new to the valley are shocked. "Your brother disappeared?"

I wait a week and then call the sheriff. "You said we'd know by now." My calls to the sheriff continue every week. For two months. *Two months!*

Finally, my phone rings and it's Sheriff Femling.

"Okay, we have the results. Come on down to my office."

"Just tell me."

There's a pause. It hangs in the air.

"It's Jay."

The truth is too sudden. What I'm hearing is unbelievable. Nine years of exhaustion start to unravel in my mind. My heart is in my throat. I fear I'll collapse on the floor, so I take to my bed.

Sleep drags me downward, and I dream I'm with some friends in a rowboat. We're paddling along on top of snow as if it were water. We get to the middle of the lake and stop. Stepping out of the boat, I slowly sink to the bottom. Lying on the sand looking up, I faintly hear my friends hollering, "Narda! Narda! Narda!" It's so peaceful, quiet, and soft, resting there.

I want to stay there, in the dream, dead.

Before Jay disappeared, depression was something foreign, an oddly paralyzing condition I knew some people suffered from. I totally didn't get it. But now I'm in the thick of it and I don't see a way out. I don't believe I can be happy again, ever. So why continue to live in misery?

Alcohol is a depressant, and depression is an illness, like alcoholism.

I'm consumed with thoughts of how to end my misery. Getting a gun and shooting myself is messy. Overdosing on sleeping pills is clean, but what if I don't die quickly enough and someone finds me? Then I'll have to go through getting my stomach pumped. Jumping off the bridge in Twin Falls would be a drag for those who will have to pick up the pieces. If it were summer, I would swim down, down, down into the water until death takes me.

How can I escape this new pain of knowing Jay is gone from the earth?

This thought of death, a place where there is no more confusion, brings me peace. My drinking and smoking become substantial.

I'm obsessed with the details of Jay's death. What happened?

When he first disappeared all those years ago, I suspected foul play. But looking back, I realize the likely truth. Jay fell from his deck early Sunday morning and hit his head. He went back to Cat's place in Gimlet, and she said he complained of headaches all day. Then he left in Cat's white Jeep Cherokee at 5 p.m. *when the rain stopped.*

But what about the man who saw a white Jeep at 3 p.m., tarp sticking out the back, coming down a road in Gimlet with rain pouring down on the man's head, because the Jeep was open to the elements?

How did Jay get all the way out to East Fork, when the Jeep was found in Gimlet?

And yet. I don't believe anyone killed Jay. Maybe something untoward happened. Most likely there were drugs, alcohol, and fear in the mix—not a combination that leads to good decisions.

I believe Jay died suddenly from his head injury, right there on Cat's couch. In the chaos of the horrific event, Cat helped Curt wrap Jay's body in a tarp, and load him into the back of her jeep. In the pouring rain, Curt drove around looking for a place to dump this ill-fated load.

My desire is to move forward, in forgiveness and gratitude for not being in confusion about Jay's whereabouts anymore. I wish the ending of this mystery could be Jay coming home. But that's not meant to be.

The finality has hit me hard. I remain motionless, years of tempered hope crumbling into weight that holds me in place.

Fall becomes winter.

Thanksgiving is gloomy, Christmas is miserable, and New Year's is hopeless. I don't want to go on, into a new year.

In early January, I get a call from a distressed parent. "My daughter is in fourth grade and can't read. Will you teach her?"

"No, sorry. I'm not involved with Nardagani any longer."

Click.

Where do I go from here? How do I heal? Stepping back from Nardagani, family and friends, I go to the mountain. In the morning, when the lifts open, I'm there waiting. The winter is cold, and nobody recognizes me all bundled up. I snowboard all day, every day, solo. Carrying a little travel pipe, I sneak into the woods for a puff. As the days and weeks pass, I cry less and healing slowly seeps in.

The next time the phone rings with a desperate parent on the other end of the line, I say, "Okay, I can help."

But who is going to help *me*? I've lost my way.

In the spring, there is a memorial service in Southern California, where AJ and Jenny now live. It's a lovely warm day. We stand on the grass not far from the beach. Dad speaks, and some of Jay's friends speak. I'm grateful to be surrounded by people who loved Jay, too.

Closure? I suppose. But I'm left with a numb feeling that lingers for an awfully long time.

Chapter 29

Finding Love

One evening about a year later, I realize Valentine's Day is coming up. Throwing a sushi party for all my single friends sounds like fun. Maybe it'll take me out of the funk I've been in ever since I learned Jay really is dead.

My friend Rhet is one of my guests. He arrives and walks into my kitchen with sake in one hand and sushi fixings in the other. As usual, he's adorable. And it's a terrific party. Everyone loves learning to roll sushi, it's the 'in' thing. When I was young and we first came back from Japan, Mom and I made sushi to take to potluck parties. People squished up their noses at us.

When all the guests leave, Rhet stays and helps me clean up. The next morning, I happen to see him up on the mountain skiing. We take a few runs together. That afternoon, he's listening to music at après ski and buys me a drink. He asks me to join him for a movie in town. My evening is open. I say yes.

We spend time together for a couple of weeks, and the next thing I know he's professing his love. We're snowshoeing on a path through the woods. It's a sunny, cold afternoon—20 degrees.

He says, "Be my girlfriend and I'll feed you. You'll never have to cook again!"

His desire for me lessens the pain in my heart, my confusion. Being with him sounds really appealing. But I'm unsure. After Rowan, I had told myself I needed a break from men. A long one.

Rhet wants to kiss me. "No. I have a rule, I must truly get to know you. I warn you—it'll be a month before I'll kiss you, three months before I'll go further with you."

"I'll earn your love every day," he says, as he slips his arms around my waist and pulls me close. His closeness feels comforting. I like him very much.

Six months later, Rhet can't stand the long drive from my apartment in Ketchum to his small home in Hailey, 14 miles away. He quotes a line from Woody Allen's movie Annie Hall: "Your condo, it's a free-floating life raft, with bad plumbing and bugs." His light blue eyes express delight.

I prepare to move in with him, with my dog Rocco and my two cats.

"I need to tell you," says Rhet, "that I'm uncomfortable with animals inside the house."

"What?" This catches me off guard.

"As a little boy, we had every bird, frog, dog, cat, horse, and even monkeys as pets. I love pets, but I just don't like to have them indoors. What I didn't like was that they all found a way to go to the bathroom in the house."

Memories of how Jay treated my pet mice surge in my mind and heart.

All I can say is, "You had monkeys?"

"We had five monkeys. Their cage was in the yard. It was chain link, and the size of a small motorhome, filled with tree branches, stumps, flowing water, and a rubber tire swing. They were woolly monkeys, very affectionate. One of the highlights of our weekly parties was to let the monkeys out after dinner. They would beeline to the tables and drink what was left of the cocktails from the glasses. In no time, they would be drunk and lying on their backs, laughing. It was the funniest thing."

I reconsider bringing Rocco and my two cats, Ghost and Jazz. "Well, after my ordeal growing up with pets, I don't want them either. We'll find the perfect home for them."

Most days, I'm still washing windows, but my being high up on ladders day in and day out makes Rhet uncomfortable. He suggests I pass the business on to someone else and come to work for him in the stonemason business. He says I could help him on the job and do the books in the office. Feeling ready to change things up, I agree.

Rhet and I get along well most of the time. Our toughest times are through the holidays. Everything triggers me, and then I get angry. Could this pattern from my childhood, all the chaos at the holidays, still be dragging me down? Or maybe the fact that I see the holidays as a family event, and my family is shattered? To be honest, every holiday—and birthdays, too—puts me in an agitated state.

My agitation increases as December 25 approaches. I snap at Rhet and create drama around any little thing he does wrong, like forgetting to pick up something at the store, being late, talking with his mouth full, or—God forbid—making a dish too spicy for me to eat. Or is he possibly being passive-aggressive? Is he subconsciously doing these things on purpose because he hates me when I'm like this?

This scenario occurs every holiday season, and leaks into other times of the year.

The only way out is *through*—processing and talking about my feelings with Rhet. But if the processing takes too long, he gets triggered, too. Then emotions escalate. I slip into confusion and depression and escape by smoking more pot and drinking alcohol. But the relief is only temporary. I'm scrambling for firm ground. I'm on loose sand, my feet sinking, and I can't pull them out.

Chapter 30

Kuna Prison

Between holidays, life is often okay. Working with Rhet allows me to focus on healing my soul. When we're not fighting, Rhet is my rock—my solid ground. He rouses me out of bed every morning at the crack of dawn, makes tea, and pats the spot next to him on the couch where we sit for 20 to 30 minutes of meditation. Meditation is so good. It helps calm and connect me with my peaceful self.

Rhet feeds me the healthiest organic foods. We hike often after work, up the canyon behind our humble home. During the winter months, we use snowshoes. Rhet and I have a loving routine of dinner at six, stretching at seven, and in bed by eight to read.

Nardagani has taken a backseat, and now I'm restless about it. I want to reach more struggling readers.

Once again, I start working steadily to improve Nardagani. I teach students whenever I discover them. I constantly talk about the program to those who seem interested.

One day, Lauri, a friend from my real estate days, comes to town. We met as agents working for RE/MAX of Sun Valley. We even opened our own brokerage firm, Mountain Living Real Estate. After many successful years together, life events steered us down separate paths and onto separate ventures.

Jay went missing during that time. I lost my appetite for the business world.

Both of us wanting to reconnect, Lauri and I meet for coffee. The first question out of her mouth is, "How are things with Nardagani?"

I say that I couldn't be bothered with it for a long time, that I needed to heal from Jay's death. "But I know I need to continue. Other people—adults and children—keep coming out of the woodwork. They reach out to me and I teach them to read. It's so easy to learn to read English this way. It changes people's lives. I love helping."

"Well, I've been thinking a lot about you and Nardagani," says Lauri. "We need to get this adopted by the Idaho State Department of Education, so teachers can use it in Idaho schools."

I think this sounds amazing. But I want to change one thing. "Let's change the name. I don't like Nardagani. It was just a name to catch Jay's attention."

"I like the name," says Lauri. "Besides, it'll cost too much money at this point to change it. You've got a website with some good video testimonials where students refer to it as 'Nardagani.' Plus, you've got thousands of books!"

She's right.

The Idaho Department of Education's application process is onerous, but Lauri goes to bat. She's tenacious, and we get accepted as one of the presenters for the spring adoption process. I travel to Boise and find myself in a room with 13 retired teachers from all over Idaho, mostly women, all of them crossing their legs, looking at their watches, and tapping their pencils impatiently. The room is cold and dim and smells like hairspray. Nobody's talking. There's a chalkboard on the wall and a large table runs down the middle of the room.

Every chair is filled except the one at the head of the table. Their eyes assess me. I feel about as big as an ant. *I can't do this.* But I push on.

I hand each teacher a small packet of papers and explain that this reading program is inspired by Japan, where the literacy rate is high. Eyeballs roll, heads shake. The tap, tap, tap continues.

The faster I teach this, the sooner I can leave. Rushing, I go through the Sound Map, explaining the 38 sounds of English interspersed with my 12 Nardagani symbols.

My impression is that these women professionals, and this scattering of men, have seen a lot of programs and products, and they're not appreciating the power and significance of my symbols.

With 15 minutes remaining, I look at the teacher on my left and ask her, "What's your first name?" I write "Carla" on the chalkboard.

I motion to the room. "Please write down 'Carla.' Here's how I code it." I write the two-dots symbol under the first "a," and the up-arrow symbol under the second "a."

"Now you code 'Carla' on your paper."

We do the same with the next teacher's name, and then the next. Halfway around the group, I realize the pencils have stopped tapping and most of the teachers are smiling. There is some chatter among them and the energy in the room is rising. Maybe I *can* do this.

"Wow, this is amazing. I've been teaching reading for 45 years, and I've never seen English broken down like this," says one of the teachers. Questions are coming at me.

"How does this work for students with dyslexia?"

"Our dyslexic students report that the symbols keep the letters grounded on the page," I say.

"What happens when you take away the symbols? Or can they only read words with your symbols?"

"The symbols are like training wheels on a bike—they help the reader learn to sound out words. Once students are confident in sounding out words, the symbols are no longer needed."

"How long does that take?"

"Our experience indicates about five weeks—that's all."

After the presentation, a woman approaches me.

"May I give you a hug?"

"Yes! Of course."

Later that afternoon I get a call to return to the site. A woman greets me and says, "Congratulations! Nardagani has been adopted by the Idaho State Department of Education. Would you be willing to do a pilot program in an Idaho women's prison?"

Along with Rhet, two friends volunteer to join us on this prison quest— Jonathan Cohen and the ever-willing Jen Rush.

An hour after breakfast at a hotel near Boise, we pull up to the prison. I see barbed wire, razor wire, and double barbed wire. Nardagani is leading me to some very strange places.

We check in at the first low cement building, show our driver's licenses, get fingerprinted, fill out paperwork, and obtain our visitor badges. A guard instructs us to park in front of the four-story cement building in the distance. We park and approach the main gate. Rhet rings the buzzer. There's a loud clank and the thick metal door unlatches. The container we enter is outdoors, a square box surrounded by endless spirals of razor wire, topped by spools of more razor wire. I look around apprehensively. The fence is 15 feet tall.

"What have you gotten us into?" Rhet whispers in my ear.

A camera is perched above our heads in the corner. The next buzzer goes off, and the second heavy metal door releases in front of us. These contained rooms are called sally ports; they're holding tanks. When the coast is clear, we can access the next area. Going into Sally Port 3, I keep looking behind me for an exit. There isn't one.

But really, what *have* I got us into?

We enter a dark, grey room and encounter several solemn guards. There are no windows and the air is stale. A guard waves us over and tells us our rights, obligations, and final warnings.

"It's our obligation to tell you that you could be held hostage inside this prison. Don't touch an inmate, stay together and always have a guard with you from this point on." I shuffle closer to Rhet.

Another guard escorts us to Sally Port 11. *Clank.* The sound echoes against the walls. The door opens and we go in. It's a long wait this time. I feel cold. A buzzer sounds, startling me. Then another *clank*, and we step out into a large corridor. Droves of female inmates quietly walk by in large groups. I feel a mixture of anticipation and fear as we wait for what comes next.

The guard leads us down the hall and abruptly takes a right. A classroom is enclosed entirely by glass. Walking in, we begin to feel like fish in a fishbowl. We have no idea how many students will be showing up.

The door opens. A guard walks in, followed by the inmates—21 in all. They file in and sit at the long, horizontal tables that fill the classroom. The women are subdued. They wear solid orange tops and pants. Looking around the room, my curiosity is piqued. Why are they in prison? Their faces are hard.

Jen, Jonathan, and Rhet spend the first hour testing each student's reading level while I mark the scores in my ledger. Their reading levels hover around second grade, with a couple of women whose levels spike to fourth. This aligns with the data I read when I was first developing Nardagani, about the correlation between challenged readers and prison rates. It almost feels uncanny.

Next, we hand out the Nardagani Sound Maps, blank pieces of paper, and special prison-issue rubber pens that are floppy to prevent the inmates from styling them into weapons. We also hand out blank nametags.

A woman with a large scar down her neck asks, "Do you want me to put my prison number on this nametag?"

"No, your first name, please."

"We don't get to use our first names here, only our numbers."

"Well, first names will be better for this class. let's get started. Hi, I'm Narda. I created Nardagani. It's inspired by the Japanese way of learning to read. It's fun. You'll see."

Within the hour, the inmates begin to loosen up. A woman missing her front teeth raises her hand. "This is fun. I never saw letters this way before."

I feel the energy in the room shift, and my shoulders release. A woman in the back of the class raises her hand. "Are we allowed to take these materials back to our cells?" I'm surprised to see she looks like a friend back home, but in an orange jumpsuit.

"Yes, you are."

The class continues for a full two hours. The women absorb the information like sponges. As we say goodbye, a big, sassy, blonde woman named Veronica puts her hand up to give me a high-five. I go to meet her hand with mine when suddenly Rhet grabs my arm.

"No touching. Sorry, Veronica. Nice try, though."

We smile at each other instead.

On the second day of class, the inmates file into the fishbowl, chattering excitedly.

"I shared what I learned with my cellmates yesterday."

"We showed our friends at the dining hall. They loved the 'shhh' symbol."

I'm thrilled that they're excited. Could it be that they are simply searching for a way to make their life in prison bearable? Or are they motivated about the prospect of finally grasping written English?

I begin to let myself hope that Nardagani really could be the answer for these women. I see how the idea of accomplishing something they never thought possible could be a veil lifted.

We planned to begin this second day with our Nardagani Bingo Game. *How will these hardened criminals react? Will they think it's childish?* Jen, Jonathan, and Rhet hand out the bingo cards and chips while I organize the corresponding flash cards we use to review the sounds and symbols as we play. To our delight, they whoop with enthusiasm.

By the end of this second class, we've taught them the entire program. They're reading our coded practice books with ease.

When the last sally port closes and we depart the prison, the air is electric with our own enthusiasm. We head to a nearby Thai restaurant to debrief.

Jen says, "Nardagani is so easy that we're done teaching and we still have another day of the pilot program. What do we do now?"

"We could spend tomorrow working with the inmates on how to best tutor Nardagani to others," Jonathan suggests. "They like teaching their friends."

Before we leave the restaurant, I point to a table across the room and say, "Remember Rowan? I was here with Rowan's brother and sister, and Charlie Brandt, a few years ago. We sat at that table planning Rowan's funeral. Then, 12 weeks later, I was back at that same table with Rowan, eating green curry."

The irony of loss and change, and expectations, has me wondering about life. What a roller coaster.

The next day, when the students file in giggling and gushing about sharing our program, they're thrilled to learn we will spend the class time teaching them how to be Nardagani tutors.

"My friend Clara will be stoked. She's envious that I get to be in class. It's refreshing, so different from dark, boring prison life."

We teach them to tutor, then wrap up the third day by re-testing each student-inmate's reading level. For testing, we use a standardized method, without Nardagani symbols. This six-hour pilot program has improved everyone's reading by at least two grade levels.

A few days after my return from Kuna Prison, I get a call. It's from Carol, the education director at the Snake River Correctional Center in Ontario, Oregon. "I'd like to conduct a Nardagani pilot program," she says. "We'll purchase your kits, go through the instructional materials you provide, and let you know how it goes."

I mail Carol two instructor kits and five student kits. Two months later, she calls me.

"You need to get out here and see what's happening."

Driving into the Oregon prison feels similar to driving into the Idaho prison. Razor wire surrounds the facility. Approaching the main entrance, I see a tall woman holding a bunch of paperwork. She sees me and begins jumping up and down. One of the files falls to the ground.

Before I can pick up the file, she's hugging me, tears streaming down her face.

"It's working! It's working! Nothing has ever worked for us before. Come, the Nardagani tutors want to meet you."

Carol takes me through all the formalities—visitor check-in, rights, obligations, and warnings. We go through the many sally ports, and arrive in a large hallway at the center of the prison. This is the largest men's prison in Oregon. Groups of male inmates walk by in denim shirts and jeans.

"Now I get why you told me not to wear denim," I say wryly to Carol.

We enter a large classroom with a bank of desktop computers in one area, tables and chairs in another. We sit down. "There are five Nardagani tutors. They should be here shortly. They're very excited to meet you."

The door opens and five men walk in, smiling.

"I'm happy to introduce our Nardagani tutors to you." They stand there, saying in unison, "Hello, so nice to meet you. Thank you for coming."

I'm startled and confused. "But you're all in denim. I don't understand."

Carol responds, "Oh, you told me that inmates could probably teach each other to read. Yes?"

Holy moly! My breath catches. This is phenomenal—the tutors are inmates! This was an idea that showed promise in the Idaho prison and Carol took it to the next level. Instead of bringing in teachers, she had inmates go through our Teacher Training and teach their fellow inmates to read.

"Okay Rhet," I tell him one day, "I've come up with an idea to make our program even easier. After we teach the first six symbols, we'll have a book written with the 12 letters that 'play fair,' plus the letters with the first six symbols. We'll leave out the letters that require the last six symbols, then we'll gradually add more symbols into the practice books as our students learn them."

I approach three different writers. They all say it can't be done. You can't write a book minus six sounds of English.

Never tell me I can't do something.

I make a list of all the words that have the easiest sounds of English, and I leave off the list all the words that include the six most complicated sounds. Choosing carefully from the many words on my list, I create a story called "Fred the Worm." My inspiration comes from my small vermicomposting business—I set people up with boxes of special worms called red wigglers that like to eat vegetable and fruit scraps. It turns out to be a humorous and instructive book. I write a couple more, slowly adding in the rest of the sounds as I go.

This proves to be a brilliant idea. Now, students are reading a short book by the second or third class. "I've never read a book before without a struggle," I hear often. Students quickly progress to the next book with more symbols, then the third book with all the symbols.

Chapter 31

My Fault

I wake with a pulsating headache and a dry mouth. My stomach is icky. *Where am I?* Slowly propping myself up on a pillow, I recognize the room. I'm in my ex-husband Eric's bed. It's just getting light outside; a cool breeze comes through the open window. Closing my eyes, my head spins. *God, I feel awful. I've got to get back to recovery meetings.*

How did I sink to this? Searching through the heavy mental fog, my memory slowly returns. Eric is out of town and I'm housesitting. His cat jumps up on the bed and startles me. I lie back down, praying for sleep that doesn't come.

My cell phone rings. Ouch, it's loud. I hear resolve in Rhet's voice. "I'm done. Please come get your things."

"What? Why?"

"Come on, Narda, after last night … I can't do this anymore."

Instantly, I sit up in bed. My mind is reeling. I recall that yesterday afternoon I checked on Eric's cat, then left the house. I drove to an outdoor concert at the Sun Valley Pavilion. Rhet was planning to meet me there, but while discussing plans over the phone, we got into an argument.

When I arrived at the concert, I found my friend, Cathie Caccia, and sat down on her picnic blanket.

"Hi."

"Where's Rhet?"

"We had a fight. He's not coming."

"What happened?"

"Oh, the usual. Two nights ago Sadie was in town, so Eric had a dinner party. A couple of Sadie's friends joined us, plus Heide, Eric's adorable girlfriend. Right after dinner, Rhet came tugging on my sleeve, ready to go home."

"And you didn't want to leave."

"Exactly! As we drove home, I was fuming, thinking about them sharing stories and laughing without me. Yesterday I was in a foul mood. The witch came out and began her usual yelling rant. Rhet got upset and threatened to break up with me. By some miracle, we managed to pull it together. Then, on the way here, we got into another fight on the phone."

"You can stay on my couch again if you'd like," Cathie offered.

I replied that I was staying at Eric's while he and Heide were away, taking care of Mr. Kitty and taking a break from Rhet.

Looking through my basket, I found a glass and filled it with wine. The announcer came on, and shortly after, the band began to play. Cathie handed me a plate of delicious food.

Cathie is one of the first people I met when I moved to Sun Valley in 1988. She's a small woman of great strength, physically, emotionally, and spiritually. Her beautiful brown hair with red highlights bobs gently around her shoulders. People are drawn to Cathie—it's hard not to be. We are two friends, trying to solve the problems of the world—and our own life issues.

We love to ski moguls from the top of the mountain to the bottom. In the summer, we ride mountain bikes. I see her as a hard-core athlete, yet she stops to take in the scenery and waits for me to catch up. She often calls to invite me out for music. She's a phenomenal dancer.

Before meeting Cathie, I rarely heard people openly say, "I love you." It certainly didn't happen in my childhood. Cathie's open affection and those three words she says so frequently seem to unlock the door to my heart.

But now, the memory of Cathie's warm presence begins to fade as I notice my dry mouth and the haze of the present moment. *Oh man, I drove back to Eric's last night after the concert. But I don't remember driving.*

Rhet's voice is low.

"You texted me around midnight, Narda. You texted, *'This is not love. I'm done. Next.'* I laid awake all night in pain. Being with you is too difficult. I'm sorry. Goodbye."

"No, wait!" I yell, checking my phone for the text. Sure enough, there it is. I hang up.

Jumping out of bed, I lunge toward the bathroom, making it just in time to vomit in the toilet.

Lying back on Eric's bed, I reflect on my life of broken relationships. I'm a pretty nice mate if not for the uncontrollable witch who comes out in a rage. The things she says are cutting, and damage the trust in my relationships.

I also have a habit of picking up introverts. Being around people, lots of them, gives me energy, while my reclusive partner feels the opposite. Men have been tugging on my sleeve my whole adult life, ready to end the party.

I'm still lying on Eric's bed around noon when I hear a knock at the front door. *Go away.* There's a creak as the door opens.

"Hello?" It's Rhet.

My heart begins to pound as I hear his heavy footsteps approach. He stands in the doorway with Eric's cat in his arms. He says, "I need to ask you something."

"Okay."

"Look, I love you. I feel desperate. Can I help you?"

Taking a deep breath, I feel Rhet's question unlock a sense of hope. But I wonder if I'm the kind of person deserving of happiness. We're both searching for acceptance, and love.

Yes, I need help. It's time to stop running. Running from self-loathing. It was not my fault that Jay disappeared. It was not my fault Mom died. I wasn't supposed to save them. If none of this had happened, all those who have learned to read through Nardagani would still be struggling. None of these miracles would have happened if Jay were still alive. I'm not a bad person. It's okay for me to have love. Happiness. *But how do I get there?*

I've been in therapy over the years. When I have the money to go, it has helped. But there is something deep in my soul that is vitally off balance. The best therapy I've experienced is when my butt is in a seat in my 12-step recovery meetings. There are plenty of fraught people in the rooms of these meetings, and then there are the angels. These wise, kind messengers bring their spiritual practice to the meeting.

I tell Rhet and myself that I'm going back to recovery.

I stop drinking and my relationship with Rhet gets better. We're in a trusting space again. I can do this, this life, with support from the recovery fellowship. I still think marijuana is medicinal, so I continue smoking. I'm sober, but not *clean* and sober.

Chapter 32

Expensive Free Help

I'm sitting at my desk in my small office, looking out the window at the lovely tall mountains. The trees are in full fall bloom, clustered together. Coding the newest practice book with the Nardagani symbols, I come across the word "flower." In order to put the Nardagani codes under this word, I must program three letters into our word bank.

I run all new practice stories through our bank of words. Each word is searched, found and then replaced, using the symbols below the "letters that don't play fair." It's the Nardagani Font. Each book takes hours of my focused attention to get just right. Sometimes my eyes grow tired. Closing them, I take 10 long, conscious breaths, relaxing at the top of the breath, and at the bottom of the breath.

In, hold, out, rest. In, hold, out, rest.

My mind relaxes and begins to wander. Visions of struggling readers learning to read with ease bring a smile to my face. I daydream about a high school girl I call "Faith." She's the girl I'm doing this for, the reason we must carry on. She hates reading because it is so confusing. Faith's school signs up for the Nardagani program. The whole school will go through the course so that challenged readers are not singled out. Besides, everyone benefits from learning this new view of English—even kids who read quite well find that Nardagani brings more meaning to what they read. And Nardagani offers remarkable improvement in spelling.

In my daydream, the 12th graders go first. All the 12th-grade teachers spend one hour, every other day, going through the program with their class. After three weeks, the course is over, and everybody is able to read, pronounce, and spell English well. All the materials—the digital part plus the exercises and coded practice books—are passed down to the grade below. That grade does the course and hands the materials down again.

Faith is in ninth grade. By the time the course gets to her teacher, everyone knows what's coming. The students are excited, the whole school is abuzz. She'll learn to read. Her school will be the next to achieve the status of 100% literacy! Faith will never again have to admit she can't read, won't have to feel embarrassed or dumb, can hold her head up high.

Thinking about the enormous potential of Nardagani waiting to be unleashed, tears of joy soothe my eyes and calm all the cells in my body.

The sound of a car engine brings me back to the moment. Looking out the window, I see a dark, four-door sedan pulling into a parking spot. A man gets out and walks across the street toward the door of the building I'm in. He wears an ill-fitting suit and a wide, shiny blue tie. He's overdressed and seems out of place. I take a deep breath. He gently raps his knuckles on my cracked door. It opens and he steps inside. His demeanor is somber. He hands me a manila envelope and says, "You've been served."

Dread grips me. A pressure builds in my throat that moves up into my head. *She did it. I can't believe it. Yvette is really suing me.*

I met Yvette in the summer of 2011, at a party she and her husband, Randy, were hosting. Mutual friends invited us to join in the fun. I remember it as if it were yesterday.

Rhet collects our go-to appetizer from the sidesaddle of his Harley—sushi, ready to slice and place. Holding hands, we walk to the front door of Randy and Yvette's home.

"Welcome," Yvette greets us. "Nice Harley!! Will you take me for a ride sometime?"

"Sure," Rhet says with a proud smile.

Yvette has short blonde hair and a gentle laugh.

After we get drinks, she pulls me aside. "I hear you have a unique way to teach people to read. I'm looking for something to fill my time. May I help you with your program? I'll do it for free!"

Oh my God, someone who has time to help me, and will do it for free!

"Sure! That would be wonderful. How'd you like to go to jail with me?" I jest, but I'm sincere about the offer. "I start teaching Nardagani at the Blaine County Detention Center next week. I'm not eager to go alone. Will you join me?"

"Yes, that sounds so fulfilling, teaching inmates to read," Yvette says. "I'm searching for something meaningful in my life."

In about three hours, I teach Yvette how Nardagani works—the program is that simple. She fills out the paperwork for her background check and gets approved. The day arrives and it's time to go to jail. Driving down the quiet lane on the outskirts of town, I think of the times I've been down this road. The first was to meet Sheriff Walt Femling to talk about Jay's disappearance. The next time was to escort Esmeralda the psychic. And now, down the road I go to teach Nardagani.

The truth is, I'd wanted for years to teach Nardagani in the local jail. For me, doing time is actually totally rewarding.

Yvette meets me at the Blaine County Detention Center entrance and we get buzzed into the front hall. Inside, we walk down a sterile hallway, passing offices to our right. We can see officers at their desks through clear glass walls. A guard greets us, and together we enter Sally Port 1. After an uncomfortable two minutes, a woman's voice comes over the speaker: "All clear." A metal clank sounds and the latch is released. The guard leads us down a hall where we get buzzed into a classroom.

Five men file into the room, wearing orange smocks, orange pants and even orange sneakers.

The bright orange contrasts with the white cinder-block walls of the county jail's library.

Paperbacks donated by community members line the shelves. They include classics like Ayn Rand's *Atlas Shrugged*, *The Count of Monte Cristo*, and Leon Uris's *Exodus*. I also see a biography on J. Edgar Hoover and various versions of the Bible, including one titled *Free on the Inside*, written specifically for prison inmates.

None of the men sitting around the table has read any of these. They've spent the first 20 or 30 years of their lives trying to navigate the world without knowing how to read. I know this without even asking.

Yvette and I sit at the front of the room. Our goal is to teach these men to read. Two of the five around the table are Hispanic. After a short introduction, we test their reading levels. Three are at a second-grade reading level, but the two Hispanic men can't read more than a few basic words. Yvette hands out the Sound Maps and we begin the Nardagani course. Halfway through the class, a big, husky inmate covered with tattoos says, "This is cool."

After four two-hour classes, we have taught the three native English speakers to read. They quickly and happily go through our many coded practice books and then test out at a grade-four reading level, two grades higher than they had tested two weeks earlier. The passages used for testing are not coded with the symbols.

The two Spanish speakers don't fare as well. On my way out of the jail that afternoon, I run into Jose Varela. He's facilitating a recovery group for the inmates. Off the top of his head he says, "Maybe you need to teach them to read Spanish first."

It's a brilliant idea. I get to work creating a program to teach our Hispanic students to read Spanish. Helen, from the Ketchum library, speaks Spanish and helps me. She teaches me the sounds of this new language to expand Nardagani. We use the English symbols where possible, then create new symbols for sounds like the rolling "r." I build all the Spanish pieces to match the English version of the program. It's a lot of work, and suddenly life becomes extremely busy. We hire Jose to become our primary teacher for the classes at the prison.

When the Spanish program is complete, Jose uses it with students. He calls me after class. "I had five students today. I taught them all to read Spanish during the two-hour class!" There is mounting excitement in his voice. "Three were Hispanic and two English. Every one of them can easily read our Spanish coded practice books!"

Once they know how to read in their native language, they easily learn to read and correctly pronounce English.

Our students are proud. "I've found myself reading because I *want* to read, instead of *having* to read. That's all thanks to your program," says one inmate. "I sure wish there was a program like this when I was young."

"It's kinda like V-8—good for you, yet tastes great," another inmate says with a laugh. "I have a new understanding of the language."

While classes continue at the jail, Yvette and I convert the room above her garage into the Nardagani main headquarters. We spend four to five days a week there, joyfully working on Nardagani.

We always have things to do, like writing proposals for implementing Nardagani in schools around southern Idaho, researching grant opportunities, making videos that show how Nardagani works, reaching out to potential investors, creating new stories to be coded, then coding them… and more.

At this point, it feels like we really have a viable business under way. There's been no talk of forming an entity because we are not business people by trade; we've simply fallen into a routine of working. There's been some talk between us of being rich and famous one day, but mostly we are focused on making the world a better place and eradicating illiteracy in our lifetime.

One afternoon my cell phone rings. It's Catherine, the grandmother of one of Sadie's friends. "You remember Sven, my grandson?" Before I have a chance to reply, she continues. "He's 12 years old… in the fifth grade. He's autistic and can't read. I met with his teachers. They told me I had to face the fact that he probably would never read." She stops speaking for a moment, then says, "Would you please teach Sven to read?"

When Yvette and I meet Sven at Catherine's home, he's sitting at the dining room table, watching TV. Catherine introduces us. Sven waves but doesn't make eye contact. I reach out to shake his waving hand and he seems shy.

Catherine says to Sven, "Remember I told you Narda was coming over today to show you how she teaches kids to read?" He seems to take more notice of me.

I perform a short test to gauge Sven's reading ability. I'm shocked to find that he can't read a single word. Not "it," not "me," not "the"— nothing. Everyone I'd taught up to this point could read a little, at least. I wonder if my program will work for this autistic boy who's starting at square one.

Suddenly, Sven looks right at me with his big blue eyes and asks, "Narda, are you going to teach me to read?"

When I nod, he says, "Well ... let's get going."

I'm excited but apprehensive. I don't want to let Sven down.

We start with the Sound Map, learning the simplest letters first. Slowly, I introduce the symbols. In between lessons, Sven plays the Nardagani games (Memory Match and Bingo) with his grandmother and his father, Sam, so he can memorize the sounds of the letters and the symbols. The silent letters are his favorites. He likes that they don't make a sound and they're easy to see because they're underlined.

school ... watch ... muscle ... knee ... ear ... right

After eight one-hour lessons, Sven is reading the coded practice books with ease, a feat that makes him grin from ear to ear. "I like reading," he tells me, giggling. "It used to be really hard. I would go someplace and see a sign and not know what it meant. But now, I even like reading stories by myself."

I feel such pride—for him and for Nardagani.

Several months later, Sven no longer needs the symbols. His father texts me pictures of his son reading the newspaper at the kitchen table. The pictures fill me with such absolute delight they send chills up my spine.

"It blows my mind to think of how far he's come," Sam texts. "Sven reads as enthusiastically as he swims and skis."

One day, about four years after teaching Sven, a local teacher named Marilyn approaches me at an outdoor summer concert in Hailey. She tells me about a time when she'd been asked to substitute in one of Sven's high school classes. A high-school-level book was being passed around the room. Each student read aloud easily, Marilyn told me, and as the book got closer to Sven, she cringed, remembering how difficult reading had been for him in elementary school. But, to Marilyn's total surprise, Sven read with confidence and ease.

"I had to turn away to hide my tears," she says. "It's such an amazing accomplishment."

In his junior year, Sven becomes a proud member of the National Honor Society of America. For a student to achieve this distinction, they're expected to "excel, serve, lead, succeed, and have a true thirst for challenge and accomplishment."

Later, during an interview with a local journalist, Sven proudly says, "I once thought reading was impossible. Now, I know all things are possible."

Six months later, Yvette and I have an opportunity to be on TV in Twin Falls, thanks to Yvette's good thinking and work to secure us an interview.

Yvette picks me up and drives us to the TV station, an hour and a half away. We check in at the front desk and then are directed down the hall to the recording studio on the left. As we await our turn, we watch the news anchor wrapping up with the people before us.

"Go to commercial," says a man into his headset. The anchor gets up, walks over and holds out her hand to me. "Hi, I'm Mitsy. So nice to meet you, Narda. I've been looking at your website. It's terrific what you're doing."

She turns to Yvette. "And who are you?"

Yvette shakes her hand firmly. "I'm Yvette Redder, co-founder of Nardagani."

Co-founder? I'm incredulous at Yvette's presumption.

"Okay, let's get rolling," says the man with the headset. The three of us get settled on cushy, peach-colored chairs around a low table. The camera rolls and Mitsy introduces us: "This is Narda Pitkethly, creator of the Nardagani Reading Program, and its co-founder, Yvette Redder."

Co-founder? Her participation began years after I had created my program. It was approved by the Idaho State Department of Education before I ever met her.

I'm silently fuming at Yvette. *How could she even begin to think she's the co-founder?* I only catch the end of Mitsy's question: "… you came up with the idea?" I share my standard answer, then show some examples of the program, which appear on the monitor. Suddenly, our three minutes is over and Mitsy is thanking us for being on her show.

Back in the car, we head north out of Twin Falls on Highway 75.

It's a harrowing ride, our mutual anger as combustible as the fuel in the tank.

"What did you mean by saying you're Nardagani's 'co-founder'?"

"Oh Narda, come on. I've been helping you create this program for over a year now."

"But I've been creating it for the past decade."

"I've been working my ass off without pay," she snaps. "This program would be dead without me. I'm tired of taking a back seat to you."

As her voice rises, so does the speedometer. I can barely breathe. The road goes by fast, but time seems to slow down as she spews cruel accusations at me. *Maybe dying while driving home from being on TV for Nardagani is an okay way to go.*

Finally, we pull into my driveway. I leap out of the car and slam the door.

For two weeks, Yvette and I don't speak. And then, like the evaporating memory of the pain of childbirth, the drama of our drive slips away. I miss my days with her, working side by side at our office, moving Nardagani forward. I write Yvette an email and ask, "If I put together an amenable contract, could we get back to our routine?" She responds that she's willing. She misses our time together, too.

My smart friend Natalie helps me draft an employment contract. It states a salary for Yvette that will start as soon as we have income. It also gives Yvette shares in the company for each year we stay together. But it lacks a termination clause if something goes wrong. *Won't we always talk and make up?*

Things get back to normal and all seems well. We secure an office in Hailey with room enough to teach Nardagani classes for local residents. But we need a leader, someone who understands business; it's time to make our busywork a real enterprise. I need to find just the right person to do this.

Within a couple days of my resolve to find help, Edmond is referred to me. Meeting him for the first time, I notice he's very serious. He's in his early sixties, over six feet tall, with broad shoulders. Edmond tells me he has a strong business background and has been searching for the next 'do-good' group to engage with. Although I don't know him well, I need someone like him, and here he is, ready to dig in. Like so many of my relationships, both personal and professional, I'm excited by this next person who is paying attention to me.

"I've looked through your website. You need to form a company, create an operating agreement, and secure funding. I'll be your CFO, in exchange for a small share of the company, and I'll get started right away."

Without a second thought, I say yes.

"Can you make this a non-profit company?" I ask him.

"It's a lot of work, not to mention expensive," Edmond says. "Since you're not a business person, or even an educator, you may want to sell your company to an education company, once we get it on the market and prove that it has traction."

I tell him I think a company with a strong foothold in the schools will reach more people. For me, the success of Nardagani has always been defined by how many people we teach to read. Now I see that, at least partly, profits will also define its success. This is a new way of thinking; I have a business to run. How will I do this?

"Well, then, let's make it a for-profit company, which will be easier to sell."

When I show Edmond the agreement between Yvette and me, he gets angry. "How can you give her so much equity? What has she done? She's worked with you less than two years!"

"I'm not a business person. I didn't know."

A week later, the three of us meet at our office to talk about Yvette's equity in the company. Edmond is agitated. "It says in your employment agreement that after four years with the company, you will get 18 percent. Since it's been less than two years that you've been assisting, Yvette, I recommend we put you in for 9 percent to start."

"No, I want the full 18," she says.

"But that's not reasonable," Edmond replies.

Suddenly, Edmond and Yvette are shouting at each other.

I yell, "Stop! Stop!"

Yvette jumps up and storms out of the room, slamming the door.

I put my head in my hands and cry.

Later that afternoon, at home, I just want to sleep. I decide to go out on the back deck to talk with my favorite tree. She's a tall aspen. Often I see faces in the curves of her branches with her heart-shaped leaves as eyes. The tree, with her many faces, often comforts me.

Walking out onto the deck, I'm shocked to see the tree lying on the ground. A jagged stump rises out of the earth. It's grey, with black around the edges, and moldy. The round base that used to hold her upright is broken into spikey spears, a sharp contrast to her trunk, which rests gently across the dirt.

I didn't realize at the time what a sign this was. A beautiful tree, rotting away over time, like my relationship with Yvette.

I wish I had taken that omen more seriously. Instead, I enter a battle with Yvette's attorney that lasts eight months, trying to settle out of court. I don't really care about the money or the shares. I just want to get Nardagani moving forward again.

Chapter 33

Resilience

Several weeks later Rhet and I are driving from Idaho to Seattle to visit my family. Rhet is behind the wheel and I've got my laptop propped up on my crossed legs. It's a lovely fall day. As we approach Snoqualmie Pass on Interstate 90, I get a feeling that we're driving into clouds. I turn off the stereo to absorb the quiet. Looking out the truck window, I notice all the evergreen trees. A hint of their fragrance drifts in on the breeze. As we crest the summit, the chairlifts of the ski area come into view. The chairs on their cables disappear into the fog. The quiet feels edgy, so different from the bustling winter.

The scene takes me back to my high school years, memories of Jay, and a wonderful time in my life. Jay was on ski patrol. He convinced his co-workers that I ought to be, too. "Our father is a neurosurgeon; medical work runs in the family. Narda is smart and a strong skier. She'll have a terrific *sled-side manner*."

First-aid training was fascinating. In a few days of classes, I learned how to care for an injured person. When my ski patrol job began, the first thing I practiced was taking an empty sled up the chairlift. I hoisted the heavy sled up under the chair and secured it. Though it was fastened on well, I felt slightly anxious. At the top, I removed the sled from the chair and maneuvered it to a stand of trees 30 feet away. I shoveled snow into the sled, and then it was time to practice going down the slope, in control, offering my snowman a smooth ride.

First-aid sleds were stationed all around the mountain. My days were filled with skiing and assisting guests on the mountain. Whenever I got a call on my radio instructing me to go to an accident, adrenaline would course through my veins. Quickly, I would head for the nearest sled. Skiing to the scene with the sled in tow, I breathed deeply, pausing at the top of my breath and at the bottom of my breath. The accident victims were usually bloody. A while back, at lunch with Jay and the men, I mentioned my aversion to blood. Now, it seems I'm usually the one assigned to crashes—lots of blood!

I'm startled out of my daydream and back into the passenger seat by my cell phone ringing.

It's Edmond. "Look, we're mothballing the company."

"What? What is mothballing?"

"Shutting it down."

"You're not making any sense."

"Look, I met with three of our mentors. We decided you're doing a bad job. You're not selling enough programs and you're making poor business decisions."

"You had a meeting without me?"

"Hey, I'm the boss now, remember? CFO!"

"Just last week I secured another investor, and we began the research study with Dr. Wilhelm," I say. "Why would we shut down?"

"Call the landlord and give notice. Move out of the office by next week. Shut it down!"

"Edmond, wait. We need this research study to fine-tune the program. Real teachers need to teach it."

"No. The decision has been made." Click.

Anger begins as a pressure in my chest. My face flushes. I put my hand out of the window and use my arm as a funnel to bring cool air onto my torso. My jaw begins to ache with the tension. *He has no right. No right at all!*

As if in slow motion, I look over at Rhet, who says, "What now?"

I release a heavy sigh. My arm rests on the windowsill and the cool air is soothing. "It was Edmond. He wants to shut down Nardagani," I say in a shaky voice. "Please drive a little faster. I need to get to Dad's to check my email."

Rhet is as passionate about Nardagani as I am. "I thought Edmond was our ally. He helped us get on our feet as a business."

My hands tighten into fists. I gently pound them on my forehead.

Once we get settled at Dad's, I check my email. There it is—an email from Edmond to me, with everyone cc'd: the mentors we have engaged from the local entrepreneurial group, the members of our company, and a potential investor. To my horror, I see Edmond has even cc'd Yvette's husband, Randy. *This is insane!*

Edmond writes that I'm mismanaging funds, that I'm doing a bad job and that he's shutting down the company effective immediately. *Mismanaging funds?* All I can recall is the investors' check I mistakenly deposited in the bank before the paperwork was complete. I put my head between my legs to stave off the nausea growing in my gut.

I hear a ping and look up to see a "reply all" from Randy. His email goes on and on about my poor judgment and flawed character. Another ping. This time, the email is from our potential investor. "Please remove me from these unprofessional emails immediately," it reads.

I feel the $400,000 evaporate into thin air, the amount this potential investor suggested could have been ours.

A pervasive fatigue washes over me. I stand up uneasily and walk down the hall. I need to lie down. I see Rhet doing yoga on the family-room floor.

"Hey, honey, what's the latest?"

"Our so-called 'ally' Edmond just threw me under the bus. I'm so embarrassed. Things ended poorly with Yvette, and now this."

"I'm sorry. I know how much our program means to you."

He's right to call it "our" program. Rhet is doing more than his share, so that I can concentrate on Nardagani. His contribution is huge—he gives me the time I need to make it work.

"Hi there," Dad says from behind me, a happy grin on his face. "You're way too serious for being on vacation. Welcome. Give me a hug." Dad is in his jogging clothes. Sweat sticks his shirt to his chest.

His face is aglow. I hug him tightly and feel my own shirt moistening. He releases first and holds me at arm's length. Looking into my eyes, he assesses me.

Looking back at my father, I see a man in amazing health. He is 80 years old. He's fit and eats healthy food. He still holds one running record, from the Hayward Classic at the University of Oregon in Eugene. At 60, he competed against runners from all over the U.S. and came in first. He still loves to compete. A familiar sense of inspiration lightens my heavy mood.

Dad lies down next to Rhet on the family room floor, pats Rhet's knee and says, "I'm so happy you're here."

I plunk down on the sofa and watch them stretch. Life suddenly feels safe again.

It's time to make peace with the past, and to manifest a better team of people for Nardagani.

I fire Edmond and keep our Nardagani company going as best I can, considering there's still a lawsuit with Yvette in progress.

Chapter 34

Angels

Early in the new year, my friend Cathie says, "I know someone who can help you. Her name is Ali Long. She started a non-profit called the Local Food Alliance. She's super smart."

"Oh, I know Ali, though not well. I'd love to talk with her."

A few days later, Rhet and I are at the grocery store. Ali and I see each other. "Hey, Narda," she says. "I was thinking about you and Nardagani the other day. There are some connections between Local Food Alliance and your practice books—they're about composting, right? Would you be interested in writing other Nardagani books to educate your students about the food cycle? Let me show you something."

While Ali digs through her purse, I take stock of this vibrant woman. She's taller than I am, with blonde hair that falls in waves down her back. I can see the muscle tone in her tanned arms. She fixes her green eyes on me and says, "Here you go." On a 4-by-6 card is a colorful graphic depicting the six phases of food, from the farm to the table: from production, processing and distribution to access, consumption, and "recovery." Worm composting is part of the recovery phase, repurposing valuable nutrients.

"Everyone should know about this system," she says. "Food touches everything, and can address so many of our problems!"

"Is it okay that the characters in the books are worms?" I ask.

She laughs, "Sure! And how is Nardagani going?"

As we move through the checkout line and walk to her car, I describe the program's progress. Ali tells me that her son struggles with reading and that if I can help him, she'll get involved with funding and support.

The next week, I teach her son Nardagani. His reading improves and, convinced of Nardagani's efficacy, Ali becomes an investor and a board member. We're off to a new start. *We have a board!*

Because of my lack of personal funds, I'm assigned a rookie attorney at the law firm that's helping me with my case against Yvette. Jacob Greenberg, an acquaintance, stands in line next to me at the post office. "How's Nardagani?" he asks. Briefly, I share with him what's on my mind and that we've hit a legal snag. He says, "Let me put you in touch with a man named Ken Lewis. He's a retired attorney and a very smart guy. He may be able to help you."

Ken, Rhet, and I meet for coffee a few days later. Ken has an engaging smile and a shock of white hair. I explain the situation and show Ken the document Natalie drafted, signed by Yvette and me.

We arrange to meet with Yvette and Randy, but only Randy shows up. Ken tells me he wants to invest in Nardagani, but only when and if this lawsuit is settled.

"Don't you want this company to succeed?" Ken asks Randy at our meeting.

Two weeks later, we reach a settlement with Yvette.

Ken invests in Nardagani and joins our board. We now have an operating agreement and have become an LLC. We hire Cheryl Allaire, a local attorney with more than 20 years' experience providing legal and strategic counsel to businesses.

Symbols LLC is official. We are on our way!

Chapter 35

One Step Forward

Who am I? I'm an artist trying to be a businesswoman. My history demonstrates my openness to including anyone who wants to join me on this journey. My mom always said, "Put your trust in people. Sometimes it will *not* work out, but most of the time it will. It's a good way to live." I've tried to follow her advice, with mixed results. But I'm determined not to let these past troubles make me bitter or distrusting.

Nardagani is at the point where a digital program makes the most sense so that we can offer it more easily worldwide. The next person in line to help is Ned, my boyfriend from 33 years ago in Japan. Still based in Japan, Ned is an app developer. He's very interested in Nardagani and seems qualified to help our small team.

In August 2016, Ned comes to Sun Valley with a proposal in hand. He meets the Nardagani board: chairman Ken Lewis, Ali Long, Rhet, and me. He wants to be our CEO, and says he'll build a team to digitize and market our program. Funding will be a "snap," he assures us. Incoming investments will include salaries for him, for me, and for Lauri, who has joined our team as administrator.

The thought of someone stepping in to lead us in this huge way feels like an amazing leap forward for our company. And it eases the burden on me.

Seeing the hope and excitement in my eyes, everyone on the board votes yes, but they tell me privately that they're not convinced Ned is the best option for CEO. Still, our attorney, Cheryl, writes up a contract that Ned and I sign.

Ned returns to Japan and begins rounding up a highly qualified group of educators and businesspeople. He retains a Japanese company to build our digital program. Every few days, Ned and I communicate through Skype. My happiness meter hits max. I have visions of struggling readers worldwide learning to read. *Wow, it's really happening!*

It's an exhilarating three months.

But, unfortunately, despite our hopes, Ned has still not secured any funding. I look at all we're accomplishing with very little funding and believe we are doing well. Oddly, my Skype meetings with Ned begin to take on an unpleasant tone. He complains about not being paid, saying we owe him for work since the beginning of August. He insists, "The board needs to come up with the money to pay me, now!" In November, Ned calls to say that for his huge amount of work, he deserves 30 percent of our company. He also calls Ken Lewis to tell him the same.

Ken requests an emergency board meeting. We gather the next day in our usual conference room at Cheryl's office. Cheryl sits patiently waiting as we take our seats and engage each other in light conversation. In the eight months since Cheryl has been our attorney, she has reworked all of our legal documents and wrapped up countless loose ends left by each so-called "helper"—the individuals along my path of growth.

Ken insists I take a seat at the head of the table. From my chair, I study Ken as he greets the others. He is a warm, large-spirited man at the ripe age of 82. He laughs easily and loves to play games, from brainteasers at the dinner table to spontaneous competition on the ski slopes. This brilliant man radiates confidence and care. Rhet calls Ken our "Bodhisattva," a person always looking out for our best interests and motivated by great compassion, who lives to bring peace to all of humanity.

Ali is talking with Rhet. I catch the last part of her story about her latest ideas for our community's food system. Ali is a powerful woman and she knows how to get things done. We all quiet down and Ken begins, "Narda, how are you feeling about Ned?"

"I can't believe the shift," I say. "I was so sure about him. Now he's quibbling about money and saying he deserves a big chunk of our company. Talk about feeling betrayed." My anger begins to rise. *How could Ned do this to me after 33 years of friendship, and three years of intimacy before that? I thought I knew him better.*

Ali pipes up. "If Ned were being reasonable, we might be able to work through this. But it seems he's being obstinate."

After a few minutes of silence, we unanimously vote to remove Ned as CEO.

I have heard that nine out of ten start-ups fail. Is this what it feels like? Am I ever going to get a break and move this company forward?

That night, at home, my feelings of betrayal fester. My breathing is labored. Steam seems to be building up just inside my ears. I feel dragged down by negativity. I think of all the time and money I've spent, and of my profound desire to help struggling readers. The heaviness of exhaustion pulls me to my bed. The suicidal ideation begins. Again. Sleep seems to be my only safe place. My favorite wintertime fantasy arises as I slip into a dream …

It's dark outside the window and the temperature is below zero. Ever so slowly, so as not to wake Rhet, I slip out of bed and dress. I put on my snow boots and sneak out the front door. Suddenly, I'm on the trail behind our house. As I hike uphill, the snow crunches under my rubber soles. I take off my jacket and let it fall to the ground. I walk a few yards further and pull off my sweater, then my shirt. The air is sharp—it cuts into my bare arms. I continue to the top of the mountain where a flat perch beckons. I lie down, putting my hat under my head to cushion it from the frozen earth. Looking up, I see stars filling the sky until they are blocked by two figures—Mom and Jay. They lift me gently and take me away.

Startled awake, I'm in bed next to Rhet. Heaviness pulls my body into the mattress. My heart aches. I long to be with Mom and Jay.

Please, God, take me away.

Chapter 36

An Accident

Depression is a mood disorder that causes a persistent feeling of sadness. I learned a technique to shift myself to a lighter level through gratitude. By focusing on the good things in my life, like how lucky I am that Jay is no longer a mystery, and that I have two independent, happy children, I can lift my mood. Life events knock me back down, but then I work to focus on positive thoughts again. Human existence is a roller coaster ride. The crucial point to remember is that what goes down, will come up.

One morning my phone rings early. It's an unfamiliar number from Jamaica. When I answer it, I see Raleigh through FaceTime, and I know immediately that something is very wrong.

"Mom, I was in a car accident last night. We slid off the road."

"What happened?"

"It was just past dark on a dangerous road. The driver, a friend of mine, miscalculated the lane and we went off a bridge. The car flew through the air, crashing into the river 25 feet below."

I can see emotion pulling at Raleigh's mouth.

"Oh my God, you must've been so scared." My heart is racing. Tears spill onto my cheeks.

"The only thing I remember was the car skidding. Just before we went off the edge, we hit a big cement block that must have knocked me out. I woke up completely submerged in water. It was dark, I was disoriented, and I had to fumble to release my seatbelt. I couldn't open my door. I felt for the window and it was gone, so I swam through the opening. I could feel my legs brush the sand just before the car landed on the bottom of the river.

"Oh Raleigh!" The images in my mind are terrifying. *Breathe.*

"I surfaced to see only a part of the car above the water. I began yelling for Rob and Simon. Rob popped up next to me and we realized that Simon was still trapped. We took turns holding the passenger door open against the flowing river and diving into the darkness to get him out, but we were disoriented and our hearts were pumping so fast we couldn't hold our breath for more than a few seconds. We each tried about three times, but we couldn't pull him out."

I'm trying to hold it together, barely able to breathe myself.

"Finally, we stopped. We figured he must be dead—he'd been underwater too long.

"Then, I calmed myself down and pictured where the seatbelt was. I swam back into the wreckage of the car. Somehow, my hands were guided to the buckle. I released the belt and pulled Simon to the surface. I propped him on the bit of car that was still above the water. Rob started mouth-to-mouth, and I pumped on Simon's chest. After a few breaths, Rob stopped so I could check for breathing or a pulse. There was nothing, so I ... I ... I started CPR again."

Raleigh is struggling to speak, his voice shaking.

"It was terrible. The CPR was nothing like in my first-aid class. It felt like it lasted forever. I kept asking myself, how long do I keep doing this on my dead friend? He was underwater way too long! Then suddenly, Simon's eyes popped open wide, and his mouth, too. We could hear shallow, hoarse breaths. Then his muscles started to spasm and he was thrashing in the water, so I held onto him with a big bear hug. Finally, he calmed down and managed to choke out the words: 'Am I dead?'"

Raleigh fills in more details of the story. He says there must have been a hundred local Jamaicans yelling in Patois from the bridge. Suddenly, Jamaicans were with them in the water, pulling at them to get onto a large bamboo pole, trying to get them out of the river.

Simon was still sitting on the small piece of car. He wanted to say something. Everyone began to quiet down for him, those in the water, then everyone on the bridge. In the silence, the whole crowd waited. Simon raised his hands in the air and shouted, "I'M ALIVE!" The swarm of people burst into cheers.

A fleeting sense of relief washes over me. "Is Simon going to be okay? Are you hurt?"

"He has water in his lungs, he's still in the hospital, but he'll be okay. I'm all scraped up and bruised. I'm just so freaked out. Last night I had terrible dreams that my bed was flooding and I couldn't get out of the water. Mom, my phone got lost in the accident, so I'm borrowing this one. I've gotta call Dad, too. I love you."

"I love you, too." I sit back in my chair in shock. My mind feels numb and I can't move.

The phone rings again, startling me. It's Eric. He's freaked out, too. With a quaver in his voice, he tells me that everything is going to be okay. There was no drinking involved. The boys were on a section of road that has taken the lives of many people, especially at night. To calm ourselves and to get beyond the jolt, we talk for a while.

Raleigh and his college buddies were thrilled to go on this trip to Jamaica after graduation, all seven of them from the tennis team. Simon and Maiz, the two Jamaican men, have been hosting the group at their parents' homes. Everyone there must be reeling in shock, too. Finally, Eric says, "I've got to get back to work. Let's talk more later."

The next morning, Raleigh calls. I answer quickly. "Oh my God, I'm so glad you called. How are you? How is Simon?"

"Simon is home from the hospital. He's okay. He just can't believe what happened. It was the scariest experience, being stuck in his seatbelt as the car sank. I can't stop thinking about the accident, and what might have happened if…"

"Oh Raleigh, it's just astounding. I have to keep telling myself that nobody died. You're a hero, you know? It's because you're a person who does what needs to be done, and you never give up."

I'm comforted talking with him, but it's not his phone and he has to go.

After we hang up, I sit down on my couch, deeply distressed, as my mind tries to probe the fear of what could have happened.

It's crazy, but during all those years when Raleigh was a pugnacious child, I would never have thought he would end up being such an inspiring adult. He is a young man who has the tenacity and the ability to save the life of a friend. What will he do next?

Chapter 37

Dream Team

It's 2017. Together with Lauri, my business partner, we continue to work on Nardagani. Our natural strengths and weaknesses complement one another. We set in motion our shared vision of helping to eradicate illiteracy—globally.

Cathie tells me on a hike that I ought to meet Ken and Morgan Martin—they, too, may be able to help. Sure enough, Ken and Morgan jump right in to volunteer with Nardagani, and they become dear friends from the moment we meet.

Morgan is a petite redhead with striking green eyes. She is smart, quick-witted, and has an adorable nose from her ancestry in Finland. She's also an artist. Her creativity runs deep. Everything she puts her attention toward blossoms.

Ken's professional background is in marketing and sales. He's sharp and expresses confidence in Nardagani's ability to teach the world to read. Ken's also a musician and loves to play guitar, mandolin, and banjo. He's in a very popular local band called The Heaters. They're notorious for attracting large crowds with people of all ages, and especially those who love to dance.

Jeffrey Wilhelm, Ph.D., joins our advisory board. He's a nationally recognized literacy expert and distinguished professor at Boise State University. Dr. Wilhelm conducted a small-scale teacher research study, in 2015, to explore the efficacy of Nardagani on the decoding skills and reading fluency rate of struggling readers in a school setting.

Dr. Wilhelm was delighted when the teachers found Nardagani easy to comprehend and to teach. Every student in the study quickly learned to read. He supports Nardagani by being a member of our team and spreading the word about our program. This kind of study legitimizes our budding company.

Is my dream team finally coming together? The thought of millions of people learning to read brings me newfound self-confidence and determination. The joy that fills me is a body, mind, and spiritual experience. My depression seems to have lifted, replaced by curiosity about what will happen next.

Patricia is a waitress at a Mexican restaurant where Rhet and I often go. Spirited and clever, she's another reminder of how Nardagani changes lives. At first, she couldn't speak a word of English. We communicated with her by pointing to menu items. I decide with Jose, our Nardagani teacher in the local jail, to take turns teaching Patricia the Nardagani way to read and pronounce English. She learns in just five weeks. Her confidence in speaking English grows exponentially. Within the year, she opens her own restaurant in town.

Before Jay disappeared, I never would have imagined my life as it is now. My focus used to be only on my family and myself. Now, my deepest desire is to ease the suffering of complete strangers around the world by giving them a simple gift—the ability to read.

To practice their newfound skill, our students read many books we have written that are coded with Nardagani symbols. Engaging and often humorous, these books are filled with insights into a better way to live, like eating healthy food, recycling, or speaking your truth to friends and in your community. We teach concepts like treating each other well, meditation and, of course, my personal favorite, vermicomposting.

Chapter 38

TEDxSunValley 2017

2016 brought the first TEDxSunValley to our area. I've watched some TED (Technology, Entertainment, and Design) talks on my laptop. The short videos always teach me something—about myself, relationships, or new ideas. The difference between TED and TEDx events are that the former takes more of a global approach, while the latter typically focuses on a local community, with local speakers.

Several people reach out to me, suggesting I apply to give a talk. Given my tremendous fear of public speaking, I won't even consider it.

The following June, my Nardagani board members insist I apply for TEDx 2017. My mind is convinced they won't choose me, and so I fill out the application. The questions guide me as to how I might present my topic and what makes me qualified to speak about it. I complete the application, send it in, and pray I won't be accepted.

When the acceptance letter arrives by email a few weeks later, I cry at the thought of standing in front of an audience and speaking without notes. Fear courses through my body. I can't imagine how I'll get from here to there in three months.

But then I begin the steps on the TEDx timeline. I start with the first one, get it done and then concentrate on the second one ... then the third. I attend the speaker meetings and every available workshop, all of which build my confidence.

I feel supported by the TEDx team members, who assure me they will hold my hand all the way to the edge of the stage. The working sessions are insightful. With input from the coaches and fellow speakers, I continue to fine-tune my talk. Getting to know the other speakers and having the opportunity to give and get constructive feedback is priceless. TEDx is all about "ideas worth spreading." The belief that mine belongs among them spurs me on.

I take every opportunity to meet with the TEDx support team to practice my talk. Erica Linson, the "TEDx angel," teaches me techniques to ease my fear. My favorite trick is to visualize the word FEAR and then see the word blow up into a million pieces.

I devote a large part of my summer to memorizing all the words of my nine-minute, ever-changing talk. Because it's ever-changing—getting more refined—it's even harder to remember.

It's September 1st, three weeks until the big day. I visit The Community Library in Ketchum and sit down with a woman who works there. I reserve the lecture hall for 30 minutes every day that it's available and ask friends and acquaintances to come listen to my talk so I can practice my delivery from the stage.

Rhet takes three weeks off work to help me, feed me, and hike with me as I do another get-ready-to-speak technique, which is to raise my heart rate while giving my talk.

Every time I walk out on the stage and practice my talk, I'm terrible. I lose track of where I am, get flustered, speak too fast, too loud, too soft, too slow. Even if only one person shows up in the audience to watch me rehearse, my heart races, my mind spins, and sweat runs down the side of my face.

Speaking in public, or even to a small group of people, has always completely terrified me. I've been in a book group of 10 women since 1992, and when everyone shows up for the meeting, I can barely speak up. And these are my longtime friends!

As September 23 approaches, I fantasize about accidents that will kill me or at least put me in the hospital. Then resignation settles in.

What's the worst that can happen? I'm a total flop, I'm horribly embarrassed, and we don't share the TEDx video on Facebook.

The dress rehearsal is no better than the 21 practice days before. In my carefully chosen outfit, I walk out on stage into total blackness, blinded by the glaring spotlights. Struck by this phenomenon, I'm relieved that I won't be distracted by who might be watching from the audience. But then, once again, about halfway through my talk, I completely forget my lines.

As I hang around watching with envy while my fellow speakers nail their practice talks, a woman I've never met before approaches me. "Your pitch is so high and you're talking too fast," she says, "Also, your pants are bunched up around your knees; it looks terrible. Just thought you should know."

I'm not sure I wanted to know.

I wake up on the big day in a cold sweat, completely exhausted. Luckily, I get to be the third speaker—I think I'd die of a heart attack waiting through any more of the 15 speakers. The TEDx angel, Erica, is waiting for me when I arrive backstage. She puts her calming hands on my back. My racing heart slows ever so slightly.

"You're up!"

Later, I will remember walking out into the blackness … then nothing else.

The next thing I know, I'm backstage, sobbing with relief. Rhet bursts through the back door. "What was that! Oh my God, you did it!"

People congratulate me the rest of the day and the whole next week. For months after my talk, people meet me and say, "You're that gal who did the amazing TEDx talk!" I'm overwhelmed with glee each time I think about what I did—how I walked directly into my fear of speaking in public and all went better than I could have imagined. I share the talk with people wanting to learn more about Nardagani. It's a way to explain, in 10 minutes, what Nardagani is and where we're going.

Chapter 39

A New Paradigm

I'm exuberant through mid-November, elated by my accomplishment at TEDx. Then the holidays hit like a brick wall, as usual. What is it about the holidays that wreck me? The logistics of who, what, when, where, and why of the season overwhelm me.

My only relief seems to come through drinking and drugs. I want to hide, to disappear.

I wake each morning, dreading having to get through another day. Quickly, I head to the bathroom for a puff of marijuana. Ahhh, the release that comes with the edge taken off. Then into the kitchen to sneak a shot of tequila. A calm seeps through my body. *I can make it through this day.*

Tensions with Rhet are at their peak. Everything he does agitates me. I release my blaming and meanness upon him easily, sharply.

I nag. "Why do we have to house your friend's motorcycle in our small garage? Can't he find another place? There's no room for my car!" *Rhet is picking his friend over me!*

"No, I don't want to eat breakfast. How many times do I have to tell you? After seven years, you still don't know I'm not a breakfast person?

"This relationship is so boring! I miss skiing. I miss living in Ketchum. Why do we have to live in Hailey anyway?"

The response from Rhet is usually, "Can't you just be happy? Don't you appreciate what I've done for you?"

Could it be that all the weed and alcohol is making me mean? So mean?
I look in the mirror and hate the person I see staring back at me.

One night, just before Christmas, we get into a fight. Rhet yells, "I'm going to get drunk!" He walks out the front door, gets into his truck and drives away.

I sit down on the couch and cry. After an hour, I call Rhet. He's drunk. I say, "Where are you? I'll come pick you up." He hangs up on me. My shame and remorse make me want to kill myself. I'll simply go for a walk in the freezing cold, lie down on the hillside, and go to sleep forever. But first, I'll get completely loaded. I head for the tequila.

Two hours later he comes in the front door, unsteady on his feet. I've never seen Rhet like this, and it scares me.

He grabs a large Mason jar full of sunflower seeds soaking in water and smashes it on the stone countertop, shouting, "I'm done! I'm done!" Glass shatters everywhere, making a wet, sharp mess throughout our kitchen and dining room. "It's your fault!" he says. "You clean it up!" He heads for the hot tub on our back deck.

I feel his eyes on me as I sweep up the huge mess. I'm a terrible person. Rhet deserves so much better. What have I done to this kind, peaceful man? Maybe I'm not meant to be in an intimate relationship.

I am haunted by thoughts of Mom, of Walter breaking glass in a drunken blackout, of Mom's death by positional asphyxia.

My neck aches and the misery continues.

Rhet never says he's sorry. He insists he's the good guy, that I'm the one with a problem in this relationship. He says he only has love to give, and it's my fault when things go wrong.

Could he be right? Maybe a therapist would shed some light on our situation. Maybe I just need some coaching. At least I could find out if there is hope for me.

On January 1, I say to Rhet, "Let's go to therapy. We need to figure out what's going on with our relationship. I know it's mostly me, but I want to do it together. We need help."

"I got therapy in my marriage," he replies. "It didn't work."

I stand my ground. "It's either therapy together or I'm moving out. I cannot live this way. My friend Dianne is heading to Southern California for the winter. She says I can stay in her apartment in Ketchum for three months if I want."

"I can't do this anymore," Rhet says as he walks away, shaking his head.

I put on my winter coat, my hat, and gloves. With my music plugged into my ears, I head out the front door toward the trail on the hillside. Before I hit play, I call for help. *God, please help me. What should I do?*

The playlist is on shuffle. The first song is "Come Sail Away" by Styx. The second is "Free Fallin" by Tom Petty. The third is "You're Not the One" by Chester See, and then comes "Glad to Go" by Four Stroke Bus.

Is God really telling me to leave Rhet through these songs? I sit in the snow looking out over the valley. I imagine living in Ketchum again, and my breathing calms. My excitement becomes palpable. Ketchum is home.

I think about a book I'm reading about relationships, and the definition of love that's written in it—a sense of feeling valued, understood, heard, and listened to. It's feeling safe with another person, with warmth in the heart and lightness in the body.

Back at Rhet's, I let him know I'll be moving to Dianne's in three days, unless he changes his mind about therapy. From that moment forward, we rarely talk and avoid each other as much as possible.

Three days later, on January 5, Rhet says, "I'll be gone all day," and slams the door behind him.

I pack up as many things as I can: clothes, toiletries, office items, and my snowboard. Fear, trepidation, and sadness are mixed with exhilaration and excitement.

Dianne's apartment is cozy, with big windows looking out to the mountains in all directions. She calls her place "the treehouse." A sweet note on the counter says, "Fresh sheets and towels! Enjoy your winter home!"

I unpack, then sit with my face in the sun to meditate. Tears come fast and hard. I really thought I'd found true love with Rhet, that forever kind of love. I had fantasized about being Mrs. Rhet. I felt content and happy with him much of the time we were together. But the dreaded holidays and the mean witch inside me did us in.

My neck hurts—a throbbing pain that began that horrible night of drunkenness and breaking glass. It stays with me as a constant reminder of my mother's tragic demise. It must be time for a puff and a shot of tequila.

Every morning when I wake, the shock of not being with Rhet brings me to tears. The crying becomes gut wrenching, like the years of grief while Jay was missing. Confusion and loss pound through my mind, breathing is difficult. Loneliness envelops me.

Rhet always took care of everything, like feeding us. Now, organic oranges, organic cereal with flax milk, and organic sautéed broccoli become my staples.

My suffering makes me desperate for healing comfort. I eat organic to heal, to let food be my medicine. I'm not afraid to die. I'm afraid to be ill. Eating organic food strengthens my body and my resolve. In an article, I read that animal products could cause cancer, so I become plant based. It's very easy to do these days.

Rhet generously put money into Nardagani from the beginning of our relationship, as I continued to make improvements, create new games, new practice books, pilot programs, and more. Rhet encouraged me to work on the program and not worry about my living expenses. Our deal was that he would support us day-to-day, and my work on Nardagani would someday get him to retirement. When we officially formed Nardagani, the many years Rhet supported me were accounted for, and the value of his shares continues to grow.

But my sadness is constant, with the hard edge of resentment. Voices in my head say, "If Rhet had been willing to go to therapy, we'd still be together, with relationship tools!" But in truth, I know on a gut level that the Universe has different ideas for my future. Jay used to tell me to forgive those for whom I felt anger. I can still hear him say, "Pray for them in order to let go of your own pain."

When I run into Rhet around town, he assures me he's doing okay, that we made the right decision, that we are on the best path. I feel this, too.

When I begin to slide back into wanting to be in touch with Rhet, I review my list of the reasons we're not good for each other. This helps a lot.

And yet … something is missing.

The winters in the mountains are cold and snowy. Sleep is my friend, and I'm in bed a lot.

One night I dream that I own a quaint cabin on the river in Ketchum. It's springtime; wildflowers are everywhere. A small vegetable garden is in the side yard. Checking the mailbox at the end of my long driveway, there's a personal letter in a small purple envelope. I open it to find a white notecard with a light pencil drawing of a couple holding hands. The note says, "Thank you, Narda, for moving on and allowing true love to blossom. Rhet and I have a calm, easy relationship. We're happy. Many blessings, Rhet's future gal."

I wake with peace in my heart.

Chapter 40

Double A

On February 14, 2018, still heartbroken and crying every day, I pray to Mom and Jay on my way to bed. I'm ready for a change.

The next morning, I wake up early. I look at the clock and it's 5:55 a.m. I'm reminded about my favorite numbers in angel numerology—buckle your seatbelt, a major life change is upon you. Angel numerology shows me a way to be encouraged by my angels through numbers.

An idea pops into my head. Instead of my morning puff, how about I walk up to town? There's a recovery meeting at 7:15 a.m. I dress warmly and walk out the door. The cold is invigorating.

Within 15 minutes, I'm standing outside the building that houses the recovery meetings and many 12-step recovery fellowships. Pausing, I think about the first time I walked through this door in 2002, the year after Jay's disappearance. I was in a similar emotional state, confused and broken, having found a way to escape my feelings a bit through marijuana and alcohol to the point where my life had become unmanageable. But I relapsed after a couple years of sobriety.

I walk through the door, down the hall, into the meeting room, and sit on the couch. An overwhelming sense of peace brings me to tears. I am home. Friends file into the room and greet me warmly. Even though I feel I've let them down, I know they will love me until I can love myself. I decide to give up marijuana, too, this time. I'm looking for real change.

After three weeks of daily recovery meetings, I feel good—not great, but good. It's a huge emotional improvement. I learn that there is also a 12-step recovery meeting for adults whose childhoods were broken by alcoholism and dysfunction.

I attend these meetings. I begin to connect some of the dots from my childhood to my thoughts and behaviors as an adult.

My normal reaction to protect myself physically and emotionally in childhood has created survival traits, compulsions, and self-harming behaviors. I have often wondered why I felt so unworthy and defective. My recovery program brilliantly, gently, and progressively unravels this dilemma and gradually returns me to my birthright of being whole. As I work this program by going to meetings and doing the step work, compassion begins to replace judgment and shame. Now, I cut myself some slack, knowing I've done the best I could. I'm removing the blocks to love and joy.

Just because I didn't feel loved as a child doesn't mean I'm unlovable.

Because I didn't have emotional guidance growing up, learning how to share my feelings in a healthy way takes practice.

I have a belief that I'm a burden to the world. This belief blocks my ability to enjoy life. Time to make a change here, too.

Chaos was normal growing up, so I emulate chaos in my life. I'm learning to be comfortable when life is calm.

Every morning I read a page from a book of daily affirmations called *Strengthening My Recovery*. It helps me start my day, knowing that I am healing. I also read the day's meditation from Melody Beattie's *The Language of Letting Go*.

After reading the day's passage, I sit quietly for 20 to 30 minutes, reminding myself to breathe deeply, and simply listen for guidance. I've read somewhere that 12 minutes a day of meditation will change your life. It's happening. My search for a peaceful existence is coming to fruition.

Since my breakup with Rhet, I've been looking for a home. Staying with friends and in a roommate situation has been an adventure, but not like being in my own place. Rentals in Ketchum are expensive and rare. Last week, I got a phone call from a woman named Julia Sullivan. She and her husband, Sean, love living here. They have a condo for rent, but instead of making the most money possible, they want to support a local person—me! Because of their generosity, I get to live affordably in Ketchum.

Coincidentally, my bedroom window looks right out on the condo where Jay lived during his time here in Ketchum. Even though it reminds me of his fall, which led to his disappearance, I find comfort in being here, next to Jay's place.

One day I'm hiking with a friend and talking about my experiences in recovery. She asks, "Isn't that group a Christian-based program?"

I laugh. "It's a common misconception. It is spiritual, but it's not religious.

"In the beginning, it was strange to conceive of a power greater than myself. I kept showing up because the people are supportive; and listening to their stories, many that I can relate to, is my favorite part.

"Then, one day, a shift began to happen. The thought that I could hand over my problems to a 'Higher Power' was calming. They say that I can have anything as my Higher Power: a tree, a mountain, Mom in heaven, the people around the room, really anything. All of these have been my Higher Power. I simply call them 'God.'

"Honestly, my Higher Power is Jay most of the time. I carry his photo, the one from the 'missing' flyer, in my wallet. When I look at that photo, I remember that whatever stress is happening is temporary. That I'll get through and that many people will learn to read through Nardagani. It's like being tethered to something bigger than myself."

I have a simple prayer I say often: "Higher Power, please guide me. If I get scared, help me remember I am not alone."

"Sounds so interesting," my friend says. "Can I go, too?"

I tell her the only requirement to come to a recovery group is a desire to stop drinking, and the only requirement to come to the other 12-step recovery fellowship is a desire to recover from the effects of growing up in an alcoholic or otherwise dysfunctional family.

In a dream one night, I walk from my condo in the dark of the morning to a recovery meeting. I'm early, and nobody is there but me. Sitting in my favorite spot on the couch, calm is in my heart and in the air.

Suddenly, friends are there—Ed, Betsy, and Linda—three people dear to me who have died, yet here they are. Jay's here, too.

I can hear them say, "We are often here, holding this sacred space. We have our own meetings, and we join you for your meetings. The calm is us."

I awake with a feeling of faith.

Epilogue

It's spring. I've been clean and sober for three months, and I am revived.

My brother Tom lives in Ketchum now, too. He works for a software company. It's a small town, and I love running into him out and about.

Our brother Richard wants to move here, too, and build a glassblowing studio in Ketchum. He's rounding up various experts in the glass world to help. Richard not only has the knowledge to oversee building a studio, he's a talented glassblowing instructor. He'll teach the whole town to blow glass!

All these years, I've kept my hand in glassblowing. I love the challenge of the art, the heat, the possibilities, the surprises. I enjoy the absolute beauty of glass. I travel to Boise, rent time at one of the hot shops, and make my favorite glass creations, Feng Shui orbs called glassy globes. I even have a friend build me a website (glassyglobes.com) to sell my art. One day I'll be blowing glass right here in Ketchum!

Visions of the three of us siblings working in a glassblowing studio together bring warmth to my core.

To honor my mother, I have a website built in her name, susanglass. com. It shows how prolific she was as an artist.

My oldest brother Dave and his wife live in a small town in Puget Sound, west of Seattle. He's a master craftsman. Dave loves to use his hands to build everything from artistic tables to houses. His wife is a talented artist in many mediums.

As for Dad, he's married to a lovely woman. Recently he called to let me know that he ran in a 10K race the weekend before.

"How did you do, Dad?"

"I came in first in my over-80 age group. First place because I was the only one in my age group!" He laughs. I'm happy his life is still so full.

The reality is that in my family, not everyone is content all the time. We have our ups and downs, because we are human beings and this is the reality of life.

The Nardagani team continues to grow and strengthen. The Ketchum Innovation Center, or "KIC," is in downtown Ketchum, six blocks from my home. I go there often for free classes to help me with the business and marketing for Nardagani. I've met mentors who have guided me, and I've met entrepreneurs like myself. At one presentation, I'm pointed out from the stage, "And look at Narda, she has stick-to-itiveness and she will succeed."

After the presentation, a man approaches me. "I'm Dan Vallimarescu. I'm new on the board of the KIC and I've heard about you." Dan is medium height, fit, with dark hair and big brown eyes. He speaks with pointed accuracy. He laughs when I tell him I will eradicate illiteracy with my program. His smile takes me by surprise. It is a full-faced grin, with adorable dimples. He reminds me of my brother Jay.

Dan is skeptical, but intrigued. We meet for coffee the next day. After I fill him in about Nardagani, he joins our board and becomes a hands-on leader. As a board member, he introduces us to talented people who are qualified to help get us to market in a strong, worldwide way. Dan travels back and forth from his home and family in New York to his home in Sun Valley.

Dan brings in Daphne Firth, a brilliant businesswoman who lives in Boston. Daphne is full of positive energy and has much experience in finance.

Cathie introduces us to Cooper Wright, an executive from New York City, who was the head of Sesame Street International. When she retired from that position, she earned a master's in digital media design for e-learning from New York University. Cooper and her husband Michael jump right in with support and guidance to help us develop the digital program. Cooper is detail-oriented and extremely creative.

We work many months together as a team. By the fall, I begin to get emails from people saying they have seen my TEDxSunValley talk and want to purchase our program. It's odd to me that people are finding the TEDx talk, since we don't have the 100% digital program done just yet. We're not promoting our program or the TEDx talk.

Going to our website, nardagani.com, I click on the TEDx video and see that there are nearly 1,000 views. Wow, how is this happening? A week later, there are even more inquiries coming in through email, and now on our Facebook and LinkedIn sites. I check the views of the TEDx talk again and they are up to 3,000! One week later, the views have reached 30,000!

I share this phenomenon with Raleigh one day, and soon I start getting daily texts from my enthusiastic son. "Views are coming in at 4,000 a day, Mom!"

I'm excited. People are hungry for our program!

I'm in my mid-50s with a lofty goal—to eradicate illiteracy worldwide. As with many people, my life feels like it's been a roller coaster ride. I certainly got discouraged along the way. I went off course a few times. I even distracted myself with alcohol and drugs. But I focused my ambition after Jay's disappearance, first on finding him and then—during the search and after it ended—on creating a reading program to help struggling readers like Jay. In this way, I feel his untimely departure from this earth left a worthwhile legacy.

I'm able to see how the worst things that happened in my life have built my character and made me who I am today. I've learned to have compassion for myself and those around me. I now trust that my Higher Power makes no mistakes. And, time really does heal. Life will be hard, but now I have tools to help me find the light.

Lately, I've been starting my morning meditation with an app called Insight Timer. My favorite guided meditation is by a woman named Sarah Blondin. Listening to Sarah reminds me to let go of my worries. She says, "We are not in control—we are floating on a cosmic river carried on the stars into our mother's womb, and then into the world.... We can allow divine grace to enter our lives. The more we trust the journey, the more fluid and joyful life becomes. Instead of feeling fear, we can feel intrigued, delighted that something new is being born every second."

As for Nardagani, I'm thrilled to guide challenged readers to learn to read in such a short time. It helps people who struggle with reading, with autism and dyslexia; it reaches inmates in prison, and people learning English as a second language. But my greatest wish is that Nardagani will gain widespread use so that youngsters in primary school learn to read at the right time, and never—never, ever—go off the rails in the first place.

Life can be bleak and foreboding for those who can't read. Nardagani offers the promise of opportunity for anyone who wants to learn.

Looking back, I see the twists and turns of my life, beginning with Jay's illiteracy. I believe his inability to read led to his desire to escape his struggle, which led to his drinking and drug use, which ultimately caused his disappearance. At first, I clung to the belief that creating Nardagani would bring Jay home. Though he never returned. When I got the sheriff's phone call right after I completed the Nardagani program, the mystery of Jay's disappearance was solved. That mystery had lead me to solve another mystery that has perplexed millions of challenged readers, the mystery of the written word.

From the darkest clouds of life, from within the most unbearable times, arise the most unexpected and powerful solutions. I miss you, Jay. Thank you for leading me to Nardagani and to the calm within myself.

For questions or to find an AA meeting in your area:
www.aa.org
(212) 870-3400

For questions or to find an ACA meeting in your area:
www.adultchildren.org
(310) 534-1815

The National Suicide Prevention Lifeline is available 24 hours everyday:
www.suicidepreventionlifeline.org
(800) 273-8255

Acknowledgements

As so often happens, many people have come into my life during the creation of this book, right when I needed them most. Geoff Affleck and Kathryn Guylay generously referred me to extremely helpful people along the way. Kathryn's e-newsletters and classes, and Geoff's outreach and courses, have guided me on how to get this book into your hands.

Kate Riley and Jennifer Casto made this entire project possible. Beginning on January 4, 2017, and every Wednesday for nine months, the three of us met to work on Jennifer's story and mine. We birthed the draft manuscripts of both our books. Without their drive, my story would never have reached the page.

Nina Shoroplova, my first editor, helped weave the chapters, so the story became more chronological.

Ali Long was my second editor, beautifully wordsmithing the text. Ali gave me inspiration to continue this quest of sharing my personal life with the whole world.

Carly Lunden, my cousin and third editor, asked discerning questions and pushed me to go deeper and reveal myself more fully than I ever intended.

Helen Morgus held my hand through this entire process. I arrived one day with my crazy idea to create Nardagani and, without hesitation, she jumped in to help. From the beginning of writing my story,

Helen eagerly read my manuscript, over and over, making notes and asking questions throughout each iteration. Helen is, quite simply, all through this book.

Patty Healey was an important copy editor. I am so grateful for our friendship and for her attention to detail. Patty was always available for a quick consult throughout the development of both this book and Nardagani.

I'd like to give a very special thank you to Ellen James for the final editing on the manuscript. Her attention to detail, her way of questioning each part, and her ability to bring even more depth to the story was a remarkable experience.

Back when my first drafts were shifting, my dear friends and family volunteered to offer feedback. Each one of them helped to improve the book dramatically: Raleigh Grossbaum, Sadieanne Grossbaum, Dr. David Pitkethly, Dave Pitkethly, Judith Glass Collins, Ken Lewis, Catherine Hayward, Sue Bailey, Jima Rice, Ken Martin, and Bob Matthews.

Thank you to my two book clubs for reading through the manuscript early on and giving me feedback and encouragement: Helen Morgus, Diana Hewett, Wendy Little, Colleen Kassner, Anne Mason, Suzan Stommel, Beth Ward, Morgan Martin, Darcy Vansteelant, Megan McMahon, Alexandra Babalis, and Cathie Caccia.

Finally, I'd like to recommend two books that, for me, were life changing: *Healing Your Attachment Wounds,* by Diane Poole Heller, Ph.D., and *The Untethered Soul,* by Michael A. Singer. My mind gets clearer each time I read or listen to them and, I feel inspired to know and to be my genuine self.

About the Author

Adventure is a big slice of Narda's personality, taking her on a lifelong journey to seek the unusual. She's a successful glass-blower, vermicompost expert, avid snowboarder, and TEDx speaker. She's the creator of an innovative reading program, which can teach nearly every person to read. Today, she lives in a small mountain town, Ketchum, Idaho, where she runs Nardagani. She learns something every day from her adult children, Sadieanne and Raleigh.

Questions for Consideration

1. Though Nardagani is brimming with unforgettable stories, which scenes were the most memorable for you? Which were the most shocking, the most inspiring?

2. Consider the problems that arise from illiteracy. How does illiteracy tie into addiction? Do you know anyone who is a struggling reader?

3. The subtitle of the book talks about finding light in the shadows. What is your light?

4. Consider the role of addiction in the book. Do you have an addiction? Addictions can be to drugs and alcohol, as well as to exercise, food, tobacco, pills, sugar, caffeine, shopping, unhealthy relationships, drama, sex, gambling, TV, internet, work, and more. Being aware of your addiction gives you the opportunity to give it up.

5. What character traits—both good and bad—do you think Narda inherited from her parents? And how do you think those traits shaped Narda's life? What are your significant character traits?

6. How is Jay's disappearance related to the creation of Nardagani? Do you believe in divine intervention?

7. At the beginning of Chapter 36, "An Accident," Narda talks about depression and states "What goes down must come up." Do you believe this?

8. What kind of man was Narda's father? What were his strengths and weaknesses, his flaws and contradictions? How about Narda's mother?

9. What do you think about Narda's description of herself? How do you feel her childhood affected her relationships as an adult?

To become a part of our community, helping people
learn to read, go to nardagani.com.

Made in the USA
San Bernardino, CA
13 February 2020